Cakes, Cupcakes & Cheesecakes

GENERAL EDITOR

Chuck Williams

RECIPES

Sarah Tenaglia

PHOTOGRAPHY

Allan Rosenberg

TIME
LIFE
BOOKS

Time-Life Books is a division of
TIME LIFE INCORPORATED

President and CEO: John M. Fahey, Jr.
President, Time-Life Books: John D. Hall

TIME-LIFE CUSTOM PUBLISHING

Vice President and Publisher: Terry Newell
Sales Director: Frances C. Mangan
Editorial Director: Robert A. Doyle

WILLIAMS-SONOMA
Founder/Vice-Chairman: Chuck Williams

WELDON OWEN INC.
President: John Owen
Publisher: Wendely Harvey
Managing Editor: Laurie Wertz
Project Coordinator: Lisa Chaney Atwood
Consulting Editor: Norman Kolpas
Copy Editor: Sharon Silva
Design/Editorial Assistant: Janique Gascoigne
Design: John Bull, The Book Design Company
Production: Stephanie Sherman, James Obata
Food Photographer: Allan Rosenberg
Additional Food Photography: Allen V. Lott
Primary Food Stylist: Heidi Gintner
Assistant Food Stylist: Danielle Di Salvo
Prop Stylists: Danielle Di Salvo, Sandra Griswold
Glossary Illustrations: Alice Harth

The Williams-Sonoma Kitchen Library
conceived and produced by Weldon Owen Inc.
814 Montgomery St., San Francisco, CA 94133

In collaboration with Williams-Sonoma
100 North Point, San Francisco, CA 94133

Production by Mandarin Offset, Hong Kong
Printed in China

A Note on Weights and Measures:
All recipes include customary U.S. and metric measurements. Metric conversions are based on a standard developed for these books and have been rounded off. Actual weights may vary.

A Weldon Owen Production

Copyright © 1995 Weldon Owen Inc.
All rights reserved, including the right of reproduction in whole or in part in any form.

Library of Congress
Cataloging-in-Publication Data:

Tenaglia, Sarah.
    Cakes, cupcakes & cheesecakes / general editor,
Chuck Williams ; recipes, Sarah Tenaglia ;
photography, Allan Rosenberg.
        p.   cm. — (Williams-Sonoma kitchen library)
    Includes index.
    ISBN 0-7835-0304-0
    1. Cake.   2. Cheesecake (Cookery)   I. Williams, Chuck.
II. Title: Cakes, cupcakes, and cheesecakes.   III. Series.
TX771.T444   1995
641.8'653—dc20   94-25663
                                                     CIP

Contents

CAKES 17

CUPCAKES 71

CHEESECAKES 81

INTRODUCTION

I've always firmly believed that you *can* have your cake and eat it too. The secret is simple: If you know how to make a cake, you'll never be without one.

It surprises me how many people today think there's a mysterious art to baking cakes, cupcakes and cheesecakes, and are thus put off from trying to make them. Only a few generations ago, it seemed that every home always had a fresh-baked cake on hand. Maybe the rush of the modern age, and the rise of convenient factory-made cakes and powdered mixes, convinced too many of us that you needed special skills or a particular knack for cake-making success.

All that most people lack, however, is a little basic knowledge about how to mix batters successfully and then bake them. That knowledge is what this book provides. It begins with a brief survey of the kitchen equipment you'll need, along with step-by-step instructions for preparing cake pans, beating egg whites, blending batters, forming cheesecake crusts and other simple techniques. The remainder of the book consists of 44 recipes for cakes, cupcakes and cheesecakes that you'll find as delicious as they are easy to make.

Armed with this reassurance and inspiration, I hope you'll be tempted to try one of these recipes right away. It's high time we all started baking more, and the recipes and instructions in this book exemplify the simplicity, ease and down-to-earth goodness of cakes, cupcakes and cheesecakes made at home.

EQUIPMENT

Basic and specialized equipment helps ensure perfect results every time you bake

Anyone who loves to bake will, no doubt, have accumulated most of the equipment shown here. If you're just starting out, however, only a relatively small investment will be required to assemble a home baker's arsenal, which will enable you to prepare any of the recipes in this book.

1. Electric Mixer
For beating butter or egg whites and mixing large quantities of batter.

2. Food Processor
For chopping, puréeing or mixing ingredients.

3. Cast-Iron Frying Pan
Ovenproof frying pan for baking upside-down cakes.

4. Hand Mixer
Hand-held electric mixer quickly beats egg whites, whips cream or blends batter.

5. Mixing Bowls
For easier mixing, choose sturdy, deep bowls.

6. Double Boiler
Ideal for melting chocolate without scorching. Water simmers in the lower pan while ingredients in the upper, smaller pan are warmed by steam heat without direct contact with the water.

7. Small Sieve
Fine-mesh sieve for dusting finished cakes with cocoa or confectioners' (icing) sugar.

8. Cake Dome and Pedestal
Raised pedestal and high fitted glass dome presents cakes attractively and keeps them fresh.

9. Muffin Pans
Tins for baking miniature (about 1½ tablespoons) and standard (about ½ cup/4 fl oz/ 125 ml) cupcakes. Whenever possible, choose stick-resistant tins. If the tins have dark surfaces, oven temperature may need to be reduced by 25°F (15°C) or baking time may need to be shortened.

10. Paper Muffin Liners
Fluted paper cups for lining muffin tins enable easier unmolding and a neater, more attractive presentation.

11. Tartlet Pans
Sturdy, fluted steel baking pans with stick-resistant coatings and removable bottoms, 4–4½ inches (10–11.5 cm) in diameter.

12. Tube Pan
Stick-resistant or standard pan with center tube that conducts heat, allowing cakes with thick batters to cook more evenly. The tube's added surface area also helps light,

air-leavened batters climb higher in the pan.

13. Bundt Pan
Traditional German-style decorative tube pan with fluted sides.

14. Round Cake Pan
Basic circular pan for layer and other kinds of cakes. Usually comes in 8- and 9-inch (20- and 23-cm) sizes. Choose good-quality, seamless, heavy metal pans. Available with removable bottom.

15. Assorted Kitchen Tools
Crockery pitcher holds wire whisk, wooden spoons, rubber spatulas and pastry brush.

16. Springform Pan
Circular pan with spring-clip sides that loosen for easy unmolding of delicate cakes and cheesecakes. Available in a range of sizes, but usually comes 9 inches (23 cm) in diameter and 2–3 inches (5–7.5 cm) deep.

17. Parchment Paper
For lining cake pans or baking sheets to prevent sticking.

18. Candy Thermometer
Heavy-duty thermometer clips to side of pan in which sugar syrups are boiled, for carefully gauging syrup temperature.

19. Wire Cooling Rack
Allows air to circulate under cakes for quick, even cooling.

20. Liquid Measuring Cup
For accurate measuring of liquid ingredients. Choose heavy-duty heat-resistant glass, marked on one side in cups and ounces, on the other in milliliters.

21. Dry Measuring Cups
In graduated sizes, for accurate measuring of dry ingredients. Straight rims allow dry ingredients to be leveled for accuracy. Choose stainless steel for precision and sturdiness.

22. Measuring Spoons
In graduated sizes, for measuring small quantities of ingredients such as baking powder and salt. Select good-quality, calibrated metal spoons with deep bowls.

23. Zester
Small, sharp holes at end of stainless-steel blade cut citrus zest into fine shreds. Choose a model with a sturdy, well-attached handle.

24. Paring Knife
For general cutting needs. Select a good-quality, stain-resistant steel blade with a firmly anchored handle.

25. Icing Spatula
Narrow-bladed metal spatula for smoothly spreading icings or other cake toppings.

26. Serrated Knife
Long serrated knife neatly cuts cakes in half horizontally for layering with frosting or fillings.

27. Assorted Cake Pans
Stack of metal baking pans includes, from bottom to top: 15½-by-10½-by-1-inch (38.5-by-26-by-2.5-cm) jelly-roll pan; 13-by-9-by-2-inch (33-by-23-by-5-cm) cake pan; 8-inch (20-cm) square cake pan; and loaf pan.

CAKE-BAKING BASICS

However a cake is leavened, flavored or shaped, a few basic principles apply to virtually any cake you make.

A cake pan is usually prepared with butter and flour (see below) and sometimes lined with parchment paper to help prevent the cake from sticking. Only very delicate batters that need to cling to the sides of the pan to help them rise skip this step.

Unless otherwise specified, all ingredients should be at room temperature before mixing. In particular, this makes butter easier to blend (see right) and allows more air to be incorporated into beaten egg whites (opposite page).

Before you prepare any cake, check the accuracy of your oven. Use an oven thermometer to gauge the heat, thus ensuring that your cake will bake at the precise temperature called for in the recipe.

PREPARING THE PAN

Instructions for preparing cake pans vary from recipe to recipe, depending on the batter's contents, how it is leavened and how much the cake will rise. The most common preparation, however, consists of simply buttering and flouring the pan to prevent the cake from sticking.

Buttering and flouring.
Using your fingers or a paper towel, smear a thin, even coating of softened butter on the bottom and sides of the cake pan. Add a spoonful of flour to the pan, then tilt and shake the pan in all directions to coat the butter evenly with the flour. Tap out any excess flour.

MIXING THE INGREDIENTS

Some of the lightest, moistest and most finely textured cakes begin with a few basic mixing techniques. Beating butter and sugar to a smooth, fluffy consistency incorporates air to help leaven the cake. Adding liquid and dry ingredients alternately to the cake batter ensures even blending of ingredients.

Beating the butter and sugar mixture.
Using an electric mixer set on medium-high speed, beat together the room-temperature butter and sugar until the mixture looks fluffy and pale yellow to ivory in color, about 2 minutes.

Alternating dry and liquid ingredients.
Using an electric mixer set on low speed or a wooden spoon, alternately add dry and liquid ingredients in batches, beating until blended after each addition.

BEATING & FOLDING EGG WHITES

Beaten egg whites contribute a light, fluffy consistency to some cakes. To beat whites to maximum volume, start with room-temperature eggs and separate them carefully, keeping the egg whites free of any trace of yolk. After beating, carefully fold in the dry ingredients so as not to deflate the egg whites.

1. Beating to stiff peaks. Be sure all your utensils are clean and dry. Put the egg whites in a large mixing bowl (adding cream of tartar if recipe calls for it). Using an electric mixer, beat the whites until they form stiff peaks. Sugar is sometimes added as the egg whites mount.

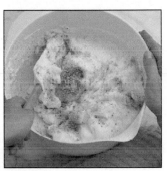

2. Folding in dry ingredients. Some batters require that dry ingredients be folded into beaten egg whites. Using a rubber spatula, incorporate the dry ingredients in batches, cutting down to the center of the bowl and scooping whites up and over. Continue to add and fold, preserving as much of the volume as possible.

TESTING CAKES FOR DONENESS

Start checking for doneness toward the end of baking time. The cake should look well risen, and yellow or white cakes should appear nicely browned; some cakes will also shrink slightly from the sides of the pan. Insert a long, thin wooden toothpick into the cake's center; it should come out clean.

UNMOLDING A CAKE

Some recipes call for cakes to cool in their pans before unmolding; others require that they be unmolded while hot and left to cool on wire racks. In either case, the following technique can be used to remove a cake from its pan easily and without damaging it.

1. Inverting onto a wire rack. If the baking pan is hot, place it on top of large pot holders or folded kitchen towels. Invert a wire rack larger than the pan on top of the pan. Firmly grasp the pan and rack together and invert them (use pot holders or oven mitts to protect your hands, if necessary).

2. Removing the pan. Return the rack and pan to the work surface, with the rack underneath the pan. Gently lift off the pan (using pot holders, if necessary). If the cake does not unmold, invert it again and run a small knife around the sides to loosen it; then repeat the procedure from step 1.

Frosting & Glazing

Rich, thick frostings based on butter or cream, and thin, shiny glazes provide the finishing touch that can elevate any cake from everyday to extraordinary. An icing spatula is all you need to apply these grace notes. As you grow more proficient at cake making, you might want to experiment with pastry bags and other professional-style equipment to achieve even more elaborate effects.

Filling & Frosting Layer Cakes

Most layer cakes are easily achieved by slicing one or more cakes horizontally into layers, spreading frosting or some other filling between the layers, and then covering the sandwichlike assembly with frosting.

1. Cutting the layers.
Unmold the cake (see previous page) and allow it to cool as directed in the recipe. Steady the cake and, holding a sharp serrated knife horizontally, carefully cut the cake into 2 layers using a gentle sawing motion. Gently lift off the top layer and set aside.

2. Frosting the cake.
Using an icing spatula, spread the filling on the bottom layer and neatly stack the next layer on top. For multilayered cakes, frost the top of each new layer until the top layer is added. Trim any uneven edges with a long, serrated knife, then spread the top and sides of the cake with frosting.

Glazing & Dusting Cakes

Whether it's poured decoratively over the top or spread evenly with a spatula, a glaze adds a touch of elegance to a cake. For an equally elegant effect, dust a cake with confectioners' (icing) sugar or cocoa.

Applying a glaze.
Prepare the glaze as directed in the recipe. Place the cake on a wire rack over a piece of waxed or parchment paper. Carefully pour the glaze over the top of the cake and, using an icing spatula, spread it smoothly over the top so that it spills over the edges, evenly coating the sides.

Dusting a cake.
Place the cake on a wire rack. Put several spoonfuls of confectioners' sugar (shown here) or cocoa in a small, fine-mesh sieve. Hold the sieve over the cake and, using a knife or wooden spoon, gently tap the sieve while moving it to apply an even dusting.

Storage Tips

Most **cakes and cupcakes** will keep well for a few days if stored in a refrigerator or at room temperature under a cake dome (see page 6) or other airtight container. If a cake dome is unavailable, place toothpicks at intervals around the cake and drape it with plastic wrap. Unfrosted cakes and cupcakes also freeze well; wrap them airtight and freeze for up to 1 month. Thaw at room temperature. **Cheesecakes,** being rich in dairy products, require refrigeration. Covered with aluminum foil and refrigerated, most plain-topped cheesecakes will keep for about 2 days.

CHEESECAKE BASICS

Cheesecake in its classic form consists of a rich, smooth filling of cream cheese, eggs and other enrichments or flavorings, baked inside a deep shell made from crushed graham crackers or cookies. To give the crumbly crust greater stability, and to ease the cheesecake's unmolding, the shell is formed inside a springform pan and sometimes baked. The pan is often wrapped in aluminum foil to prevent seepage.

MAKING A CRUMB CRUST

All crumb crusts include graham crackers or other crisp cookies, along with butter and sugar. Other ingredients such as nuts, coconut or citrus zest are sometimes added to enhance the taste and texture.

1. Mixing the crust.
Put the crust ingredients in a food processor fitted with the metal blade and process until they begin to stick together.

2. Forming the crust.
Drape plastic wrap over your hand to form a glove and press the crumb mixture firmly and evenly into a springform pan. If directed, bake the crust for 10 minutes. Let the crust cool before filling it.

WORKING WITH GELATIN

Unflavored gelatin may be added to lighter, unbaked cheesecake fillings that require additional body, enabling them to be sliced and served neatly. Before use, powdered gelatin must be dissolved in water.

1. Sprinkling in the gelatin.
Put the amount of water specified in the recipe in a small saucepan. Sprinkle powdered unflavored gelatin evenly over the water and let soften for 5 minutes.

2. Dissolving the gelatin.
Stir the gelatin over low heat until it is completely dissolved (as shown at left) before proceeding with the filling's preparation.

Classic Lemon Cheesecake

Butter Pound Cake

This dense, buttery cake with a deep brown crust takes its name from the fact that it was traditionally made with 1 pound (500 g) each butter, flour, sugar and eggs. Here is a smaller version of this favorite cake that is just as wonderfully rich. It can be stored in a lock-top plastic bag at room temperature for up to 2 days.

3 large eggs, at room temperature
1½ teaspoons vanilla extract (essence)
1½ cups (6 oz/185 g) cake (soft-wheat) flour
¾ teaspoon baking powder
¼ teaspoon salt
¾ cup (6 oz/185 g) unsalted butter, at room temperature
¾ cup (6 oz/185 g) sugar

Position a rack in the middle of an oven and preheat to 350°F (180°C). Butter and flour an 8½-by-4½-by-2½-inch (21-by-11-by-6-cm) loaf pan (6-cup/48-fl oz/1.5-l capacity).

In a medium bowl, whisk together the eggs and vanilla extract until blended. In a small bowl, sift together the flour, baking powder and salt. In a large bowl, using an electric mixer set on medium-high speed, beat the butter until light. Gradually add the sugar, beating until fluffy and ivory colored. Then gradually beat in the egg mixture until well mixed.

Reduce the speed to low and gradually beat in the flour mixture, occasionally scraping down the sides of the bowl, just until combined. Do not overmix. Transfer the batter to the prepared pan and smooth the top with a rubber spatula.

Bake until the top is deep golden brown and a toothpick inserted into the center comes out clean, about 1 hour and 10 minutes. Transfer to a rack and let cool in the pan for 10 minutes. Invert onto the rack, turn right-side up and let cool completely.

Makes 1 loaf cake; serves 8

Butter Pound Cake

Vanilla Buttercream

Buttercream is a classic French frosting that is used to ice a variety of cakes and meringues.

⅔ cup (5 oz/155 g) sugar
4 large egg yolks, at room temperature
1 tablespoon water
1 cup (8 oz/250 g) unsalted butter, at room temperature, cut into tablespoon-sized pieces
1½ teaspoons vanilla extract (essence)

In a medium-sized metal bowl, whisk together the sugar, egg yolks and water. Set the bowl over a saucepan of simmering water. Do not allow the bottom of the bowl to touch the water. Whisk constantly until the mixture registers 170°F (77°C) on a candy thermometer, about 4 minutes.

Remove the bowl from over the water. Using an electric mixer set on high speed, beat the egg mixture until cool and thick, about 5 minutes. Gradually add the butter, about 1 tablespoon at a time, beating until smooth after each addition. Beat in the vanilla extract. If the buttercream appears broken or lumpy, set the bowl back over simmering water for a few seconds, then beat again until smooth.

To store, cover and refrigerate for up to 2 days. Before using, let stand at room temperature until softened. If necessary, rewarm over a saucepan of simmering water for a few seconds, then beat until smooth.

Makes about 2⅓ cups (19 fl oz/580 ml)

For coconut flavor: Omit the water and whisk in 3 tablespoons canned sweetened cream of coconut with the sugar and egg yolks. Then add 1 teaspoon imitation coconut extract (essence) with the vanilla extract. Mix ½ cup (1½ oz/45 g) toasted sweetened shredded coconut (*see glossary, page 105*) into the finished buttercream.

For coffee flavor: Stir in 2 teaspoons instant espresso powder when the cooked egg mixture is removed from the heat, then beat as directed.

For orange flavor: Add 1 tablespoon grated orange zest with the vanilla extract.

For vanilla bean flavor: Cut 1 vanilla bean in half lengthwise and, using the tip of a sharp knife, scrape the seeds from the bean into the finished buttercream; beat in the seeds to distribute evenly.

Vanilla Buttercream

Cream Cheese Frosting

Spread this popular frosting over carrot cake (page 33) or on any cake where a rich, tangy frosting is desirable.

1 lb (500 g) cream cheese, at room temperature
6 tablespoons (3 oz/90 g) unsalted butter, at room
   temperature
1¼ cups (5 oz/155 g) confectioners' (icing) sugar
1½ teaspoons vanilla extract (essence)

*I*n a large bowl, combine the cream cheese and butter. Using an electric mixer set on medium-high speed, beat until smooth. Reduce the speed to low, add the confectioners' sugar and again beat until smooth. Beat in the vanilla extract until well blended.

   To store, cover and refrigerate for up to 1 week. Bring to room temperature before using.

Makes about 2¾ cups (22 fl oz/680 ml)

For almond flavor: Add 1½ teaspoons almond extract (essence) with the vanilla extract.

For orange flavor: Add 2 tablespoons undiluted thawed, frozen orange juice concentrate and 1½ teaspoons grated orange zest with the vanilla extract.

For coconut flavor: Bring 1 can (15 fl oz/470 ml) sweetened cream of coconut to a boil in a large, heavy saucepan. Reduce the heat to low and simmer without stirring for 10 minutes. You should have about 1 cup (8 fl oz/250 ml). Remove from the heat and refrigerate for 1 hour until cool, then beat the cooled coconut cream into the finished frosting. Add 1 cup (3 oz/90 g) toasted sweetened shredded coconut (*see glossary, page 105*) and beat until fully combined. This will yield 4 cups (32 fl oz/1 l) frosting. For an easier coconut-flavored frosting, beat 1½ teaspoons imitation coconut extract (essence) and the 1 cup (3 oz/90 g) toasted coconut into the finished plain cream cheese frosting.

Confectioners' Sugar Icing

An old-fashioned, versatile and easy-to-make icing that can be drizzled or spread over cakes.

¼ cup (2 oz/60 g) unsalted butter
1 tablespoon water
½ cup (2 oz/60 g) confectioners' (icing) sugar

*I*n a small saucepan over medium heat, stir together the butter and water until the butter melts. Remove from the heat and let stand until cool, about 5 minutes.

   Add the sugar to the butter mixture and whisk vigorously until smooth and thickened, about 1 minute. Use within 5 minutes, or the icing may become too thick to drizzle. If the icing does become too thick, rewarm it for 2 or 3 seconds over low heat, whisking constantly.

Makes a scant ½ cup (4 fl oz/125 ml)

For orange flavor: Use 1 tablespoon undiluted thawed, frozen orange juice concentrate in place of the water.

For brown sugar flavor: Add ¼ cup (2 oz/60 g) firmly packed brown sugar to the warm butter mixture and stir until the sugar dissolves; let cool, then whisk in the confectioners' sugar.

For clove flavor: Add ⅛ teaspoon ground cloves with the confectioners' sugar.

For lime or lemon flavor: Use 1 tablespoon fresh lime or lemon juice in place of the water and add ½ teaspoon grated lime or lemon zest with the confectioners' sugar.

Confectioners' Sugar Icing

Cream Cheese Frosting

Bittersweet Chocolate Glaze

This simple glaze is used on many French cakes when a thin, shiny coating is desired. If you like, whisk in 1 tablespoon Cognac or rum once the chocolate melts.

6 tablespoons (3 fl oz/90 ml) heavy (double) cream
6 tablespoons (3 fl oz/90 ml) dark corn syrup
8 oz (250 g) bittersweet chocolate, chopped

In a medium-sized, heavy saucepan over medium heat, combine the cream and corn syrup. Bring to a simmer, then reduce the heat to low. Add the chocolate and whisk until melted and smooth, about 1 minute.

Remove from the heat and let stand until lukewarm, about 10 minutes. The glaze should be thick but still pourable.

Makes about 1⅓ cups (11 fl oz/330 ml)

For raspberry flavor: Increase the cream to ½ cup (4 fl oz/125 ml) and use 6 tablespoons (3 oz/90 g) seedless raspberry jam in place of the corn syrup.

For topping cheesecake: Omit the corn syrup and increase the cream to ¾ cup (6 fl oz/180 ml).

Sour Cream Fudge Frosting

Here is a luscious, silky-textured frosting that complements a number of the recipes in this book, including chocolate layer cake (recipe on page 51), Almond Roca cake (page 60), golden cake (page 67) and chocolate cupcakes with peppermint fudge frosting (page 71).

¼ cup (2 oz/60 g) unsalted butter
¼ cup (2 fl oz/60 ml) heavy (double) cream
10 oz (315 g) bittersweet chocolate, chopped
¾ cup (6 fl oz/180 ml) sour cream
1 cup (4 oz/125 g) confectioners' (icing) sugar

In a medium-sized, heavy saucepan over low heat, combine the butter and cream. Heat, stirring frequently, until the butter melts. Add the chocolate and whisk until melted and smooth, about 2 minutes. Remove from the heat; let cool to barely lukewarm, about 8 minutes.

Whisk in the sour cream until fully combined. Then whisk in the confectioners' sugar. Let stand until thick enough to spread, about 10 minutes. If the frosting becomes too stiff to spread, rewarm briefly over low heat and whisk again until smooth.

Makes about 2⅔ cups (21 fl oz/660 ml)

For mocha flavor: Add 1 tablespoon instant espresso powder or regular coffee powder to the butter and cream.

For peppermint flavor: Whisk ½ teaspoon peppermint extract (essence) into the frosting before adding the confectioners' sugar.

For tangerine flavor: Whisk 1 tablespoon grated tangerine zest into the frosting before adding the confectioners' sugar.

Bittersweet Chocolate Glaze

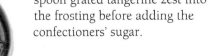

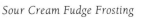

Sour Cream Fudge Frosting

Polenta–Vanilla Bean Cake

1¼ cups (5 oz/155 g) cake (soft-wheat)
   flour
⅔ cup (3½ oz/105 g) yellow cornmeal
½ teaspoon baking powder
¼ teaspoon salt
¾ cup (6 oz/185 g) unsalted butter, at
   room temperature
1 vanilla bean, cut in half lengthwise
1 cup (8 oz/250 g) sugar
3 large eggs, at room temperature

Cornmeal, also known as polenta, contributes a pleasant crunch to this fragrant cake. If you like, serve slices of the cake with sweetened whipped cream and lightly sweetened fresh boysenberries, blackberries or peach slices spooned over the top.

Position a rack in the middle of an oven and preheat to 350°F (180°C). Butter and flour an 8½-by-4½-by-2½-inch (21-by-11-by-6-cm) loaf pan (6-cup/48-fl oz/1.5-l capacity).

In a medium bowl, stir together the flour, cornmeal, baking powder and salt. Set aside. Place the butter in a large bowl. Using a knife, scrape out the seeds from the vanilla bean into the bowl holding the butter. Using an electric mixer set on medium-high speed, beat the butter until light. Gradually add the sugar, beating until fluffy and ivory colored, about 2 minutes. Add the eggs, one at a time, beating well after each addition. Reduce the speed to low and gradually beat in the flour mixture just until combined. Transfer the batter to the prepared pan and smooth the top with a rubber spatula.

Bake until a toothpick inserted into the center comes out clean, about 1¼ hours. Transfer to a rack and let cool in the pan for 10 minutes. Invert onto the rack, turn rightside up and let cool completely.

Serve immediately, or store in a lock-top plastic bag at room temperature for up to 1 day.

Makes 1 loaf cake; serves 8

Almond-Scented White Cake

2 cups (10 oz/315 g) unbleached
   all-purpose (plain) flour
1 tablespoon baking powder
½ teaspoon salt
¾ cup (6 oz/185 g) unsalted butter,
   at room temperature
1½ cups (12 oz/375 g) sugar
2 teaspoons vanilla extract (essence)
1 teaspoon almond extract (essence)
1 cup (8 fl oz/250 ml) milk
5 large egg whites, at room temperature
cream cheese frosting flavored with
   almond (recipe on page 14)
¾ cup (7½ oz/235 g) raspberry
   preserves, melted
raspberries, optional
1¼ cups (5 oz/155 g) sliced almonds,
   lightly toasted (see glossary, page 106)
   and cooled

Position a rack in the middle of an oven and preheat to 350°F (180°C). Butter and flour 2 round cake pans each 9 inches (23 cm) in diameter and 1½ inches (4 cm) deep.

In a medium bowl, sift together the flour, baking powder and salt. In a large bowl, using an electric mixer set on medium-high speed, beat the butter until light. Gradually add the sugar, beating until well blended. Beat in the vanilla and almond extracts. Reduce the speed to low and, dividing the flour mixture into 3 batches, beat the flour mixture into the butter mixture alternately with the milk just until combined.

In a large bowl, using an electric mixer fitted with clean, dry beaters and set on high speed, beat the egg whites until stiff peaks form. Using a rubber spatula, gently fold the beaten whites into the batter just until incorporated. Divide the batter between the prepared pans; smooth with the spatula.

Bake until a toothpick inserted into the centers comes out clean, about 30 minutes. Transfer to racks and let cool in the pans for 10 minutes. Run a sharp knife around the pan sides to loosen the cakes. Invert onto racks and let cool completely.

Using a long serrated knife, cut each cake in half horizontally. Place 1 layer on a plate. Spread ½ cup (4 fl oz/125 ml) of the frosting over the top, then drizzle on ¼ cup (2 fl oz/60 ml) of the melted preserves. Top with another layer and repeat with the same amounts of frosting and preserves. Top with a third layer and again repeat with the same amounts of frosting and preserves. Top with the fourth cake layer, cut side down. Spread the remaining frosting over the top and sides. Ring the top with raspberries, if desired, and press the toasted almonds onto the sides.

Serve immediately, or cover with a cake dome and refrigerate for up to 1 day. Bring to room temperature before serving.

Makes one 9-inch (23-cm) cake; serves 10–12

Espresso Tiramisù

3 cups (1½ lb/750 g) mascarpone
  cheese
1½ cups (6 oz/185 g) confectioners'
  (icing) sugar
¼ cup (2 fl oz/60 ml) Marsala
¾ cup (6 fl oz/180 ml) heavy (double)
  cream, chilled
⅔ cup (5 fl oz/160 ml) water
5 teaspoons instant espresso powder or
  regular coffee powder
butter pound cake, homemade *(recipe
  on page 12)* or store-bought
unsweetened cocoa

*Tiramisù (literally, "pick me up") is an Italian dessert that has
become highly popular in recent years. It is traditionally made
with ladyfingers, but pound cake works well too. If you can't find
mascarpone, substitute 1 ½ pounds (750 g) light cream cheese
blended with ½ cup (4 fl oz/125 ml) heavy (double) cream and
6 tablespoons (3 fl oz/90 ml) sour cream.*

*I*n a medium bowl, using an electric mixer set on medium
speed, beat together the mascarpone cheese, 1 cup (4 oz/125 g)
of the confectioners' sugar and the Marsala until well blended.
Add the cream and beat until fluffy, about 1 minute. Set aside.

In a small, heavy saucepan over high heat, combine the water,
the remaining ½ cup (2 oz/60 g) confectioners' sugar and the
espresso or coffee powder. Bring to a boil, stirring occasionally.
Remove from the heat and let cool.

Using a long serrated knife, cut the cake crosswise into slices
¼–⅓ inch (6–9 mm) thick. Select a 2½-qt (2.5-l) oval or rectan-
gular glass or ceramic dish about 11 inches (28 cm) in diameter
and 2 inches (5 cm) deep. Arrange enough of the cake slices in a
single layer over the bottom of the dish to cover completely,
trimming to fit as needed. Brush half of the cooled espresso syrup
over the cake. Spread half of the cheese mixture evenly over the
top. Top with enough of the cake slices in a single layer to cover
completely, trimming to fit as needed. Brush the remaining
cooled espresso syrup evenly over the top. Then spread the
remaining cheese mixture over the top. Cover with plastic wrap
and refrigerate until firm, at least 2 hours or for up to 2 days.

Using a fine-mesh sieve, sift cocoa evenly over the top just
before serving. Using a large spoon, scoop the tiramisù onto
individual plates.

Serves 10–12

Gingerbread with Crystallized Ginger

1½ cups (7½ oz/235 g) unbleached all-purpose (plain) flour

1 teaspoon ground cinnamon

¾ teaspoon ground ginger

½ teaspoon baking powder

½ teaspoon baking soda (bicarbonate of soda)

½ teaspoon salt

½ cup (4 oz/125 g) unsalted butter, at room temperature

½ cup (3½ oz/105 g) firmly packed brown sugar

1 large egg

½ cup (4 fl oz/125 ml) light (unsulfured) molasses

½ cup (4 fl oz/125 ml) apple juice

¼ cup (½ oz/15 g) chopped crystallized ginger

confectioners' (icing) sugar, optional

The optional confectioners' sugar topping can also be stenciled on the cake: Cut out paper into the desired designs, place on the cake and sift the sugar over the cutouts until they are evenly coated, then carefully lift off the paper.

Position a rack in the middle of an oven and preheat to 350°F (180°C). Butter and flour an 8-inch (20-cm) square baking pan with 2-inch (5-cm) sides.

In a medium bowl, sift together the flour, cinnamon, ginger, baking powder, baking soda and salt. In a large bowl, using an electric mixer set on medium-high speed, beat the butter until light. Add the brown sugar and beat until fluffy, about 2 minutes. Add the egg and molasses and beat until well blended. Reduce the speed to low and, dividing the flour mixture into 3 batches, beat the flour mixture into the butter mixture alternately with the apple juice, beginning and ending with the flour mixture. Stir in the crystallized ginger. Spoon the batter into the prepared pan.

Bake until a toothpick inserted into the center comes out clean, about 35 minutes. Transfer to a rack and let cool in the pan for 20 minutes. Invert onto the rack, turn right-side up and transfer to a serving plate.

Using a fine-mesh sieve, sift confectioners' sugar evenly over the cake just before serving, if desired. Serve warm or at room temperature, cut into squares. Alternatively, let the cake cool completely, wrap in aluminum foil and let stand at room temperature for up to 1 day before serving. Sift confectioners' sugar over the cake just before serving, if desired.

Makes one 8-inch (20-cm) cake; serves 9

Orange Layer Cake

2½ cups (10 oz/315 g) cake (soft-wheat) flour

¾ teaspoon baking powder

¼ teaspoon baking soda (bicarbonate of soda)

¾ cup (6 oz/185 g) unsalted butter, at room temperature

1⅓ cups (11 oz/330 g) sugar

2 teaspoons grated orange zest

1 teaspoon vanilla extract (essence)

4 large eggs, at room temperature

½ cup (4 fl oz/125 ml) milk

¼ cup (2 fl oz/60 ml) undiluted thawed, frozen orange juice concentrate

cream cheese frosting flavored with orange (*recipe on page 14*)

For a pretty garnish, thinly slice an orange, then cut the slices in half and press them, curved side up, firmly against the bottom edge of the cake. To add a more intense orange flavor, brush 2 tablespoons Grand Marnier or Cointreau over each cake layer before spreading on the frosting.

Position a rack in the middle of an oven and preheat to 350°F (180°C). Butter and flour 2 round cake pans each 9 inches (23 cm) in diameter and 1½ inches (4 cm) deep.

In a small bowl, sift together the flour, baking powder and baking soda. In a large bowl, using an electric mixer set on medium-high speed, beat together the butter and sugar until fluffy and ivory colored, about 2 minutes. Beat in the orange zest and vanilla extract. Add the eggs, one at a time, beating well after each addition. Reduce the speed to low and, dividing the flour mixture into 3 batches, beat the flour mixture into the butter mixture alternately with the milk and orange juice concentrate, beginning and ending with the flour mixture. Divide the batter evenly between the prepared pans.

Bake until a toothpick inserted into the centers comes out clean, about 25 minutes. Transfer to racks and let cool in the pans for 10 minutes. Invert onto the racks, turn right-side up and let cool completely.

Place 1 cake layer on a plate. Spread 1¼ cups (10 fl oz/310 ml) of the frosting over the top. Place the second cake layer on top. Spread the remaining frosting over the top and sides of the cake. Serve immediately, or cover with a cake dome and refrigerate for up to 1 day. Bring to room temperature before serving.

Makes one 9-inch (23-cm) cake; serves 12

Flourless Chocolate Cake

10 oz (315 g) bittersweet chocolate,
  chopped
¾ cup (6 oz/185 g) unsalted butter,
  cut into pieces
2 teaspoons vanilla extract (essence)
5 large eggs, at room temperature
1 cup (8 oz/250 g) sugar
bittersweet chocolate glaze (recipe on
  page 15)

As this cake bakes, it rises like a soufflé and then falls as it cools. If desired, press 1 cup (5 oz/155 g) chopped toasted hazelnuts (filberts) or macadamia nuts onto the sides of the freshly glazed cake.

Position a rack in the middle of an oven and preheat to 350°F (180°C). Butter a springform pan 9 inches (23 cm) in diameter and 3 inches (7.5 cm) deep. Line the pan bottom with a piece of parchment paper cut to fit precisely.

In a heavy saucepan over medium-low heat, combine the chocolate and butter. Heat, stirring, until the mixture is smooth. Remove from the heat and let cool. Whisk in the vanilla.

In a large bowl, combine the eggs and sugar. Using an electric mixer set on medium-high speed, beat until the mixture lightens and triples in volume, about 6 minutes. Pour the chocolate mixture over the egg mixture. Using a rubber spatula, gently fold them together. Pour the batter into the prepared pan.

Bake until the top forms a crust and cracks and a toothpick inserted into the center comes out with some wet batter attached, about 45 minutes. Transfer to a rack. Immediately run a knife around the pan sides to loosen the cake; it will fall in the center. Press down on the edges to even the top. Let cool.

Release the pan sides and remove them. Trim off any crumbly edges. Invert a flat plate over the cake and invert them together. Lift off the pan bottom and peel off the parchment paper. Tuck strips of waxed or parchment paper under the edges of the cake and pour the lukewarm glaze over the cake top; use an icing spatula to coax it down the sides. When the glaze stops dripping, remove the paper. Refrigerate until the glaze sets, about 1 hour.

Serve immediately, or cover with a cake dome and refrigerate for up to 1 week. Serve cold or at room temperature.

Makes one 9-inch (23-cm) cake; serves 12–14

Hazelnut-Raspberry Torte

2 cups (10 oz/315 g) hazelnuts
  (filberts), lightly toasted (*see glossary,
  page 106*) and cooled
1⅔ cups (13 oz/400 g) granulated
  sugar
⅓ cup (2 oz/60 g) unbleached all-
  purpose (plain) flour
¼ teaspoon salt
6 large eggs, separated, at room
  temperature
5 tablespoons (2½ oz/75 g) unsalted
  butter, melted and kept warm
½ teaspoon cream of tartar
bittersweet chocolate glaze flavored
  with raspberry (*recipe on page 15*)
2 cups (8 oz/250 g) raspberries
confectioners' (icing) sugar

Position a rack in the middle of an oven and preheat to 350°F (180°C). Butter and flour a 15½-by-10½-by-1-inch (38.5-by-26-by-2.5-cm) jelly-roll pan. Line the bottom with parchment paper cut to fit precisely.

In a food processor fitted with the metal blade, combine the hazelnuts, ⅔ cup (5 oz/150 g) of the granulated sugar, the flour and salt. Process to grind finely. Set aside. In a large bowl, whisk together the egg yolks and the remaining 1 cup (8 oz/250 g) granulated sugar until blended. Whisk in the warm butter.

In a large bowl, using an electric mixer set on high speed, beat together the egg whites and cream of tartar until stiff peaks form. Whisk one-third of the nut mixture into the yolk mixture. Then, using a rubber spatula, fold in one-third of the beaten whites. Again, fold in one-third of the nut mixture, and then one-third of the whites. Fold in the remaining nut mixture and then the remaining whites. Do not overmix. Transfer to the prepared pan; smooth the top with the spatula.

Bake until a toothpick inserted into the center comes out clean, about 20 minutes. Transfer to a rack and let cool completely in the pan.

Run a knife around the pan sides to loosen the cake. Invert onto a work surface; peel off the parchment. Cut the cake crosswise into 3 strips each about 10 by 5 inches (25 by 13 cm). Place 1 strip on a platter. Spread ⅓ cup (3 fl oz/80 ml) of the glaze on top. Place a second cake strip on top of the first. Spread ⅓ cup (3 fl oz/80 ml) glaze on top. Place the third cake strip on top. Spread the remaining glaze over the top and sides of the cake and arrange the raspberries on top. Let stand until the glaze sets, about 1 hour. Using a fine-mesh sieve, sift confectioners' sugar evenly over the berries just before serving.

Makes one 10-by-5-inch (25-by-13-cm) cake; serves 12

Cranberry-Cherry Cake

3 cups (12 oz/375 g) cake (soft-wheat)
  flour
1½ teaspoons baking soda (bicarbonate
  of soda)
½ teaspoon salt
1½ cups (12 oz/375 g) sugar
½ cup (4 oz/125 g) unsalted butter,
  melted and cooled
2 large eggs, at room temperature
1 teaspoon grated lemon zest
1¼ cups (10 fl oz/310 ml) buttermilk
1½ cups (6 oz/185 g) fresh or frozen
  cranberries
1 cup (4 oz/125 g) dried pitted cherries
confectioners' sugar icing flavored with
  clove (recipe on page 14)

Add this festive cake to your breakfast or brunch menu for Christmas morning—or any morning of the year. Chopped dried apricots or golden raisins (sultanas) can be substituted for the dried cherries.

*P*osition a rack in the middle of an oven and preheat to 350°F (180°C). Butter a 2½-qt (2½-l) nonstick bundt pan 10 inches (25 cm) in diameter and 3 inches (7.5 cm) deep.

In a medium bowl, sift together the flour, baking soda and salt. In a large bowl, whisk together the sugar, melted butter, eggs and lemon zest until well blended. Dividing the flour mixture into 3 batches, whisk the flour mixture into the sugar mixture alternately with the buttermilk, beginning and ending with the flour mixture. Fold in the cranberries and cherries. Transfer the batter to the prepared pan.

Bake until a toothpick inserted near the center comes out clean, about 50 minutes. Transfer to a rack and let cool in the pan for 10 minutes. Invert the cake onto the rack and let cool completely. Transfer to a plate and drizzle the icing evenly over the cooled cake, allowing it to run over the sides slightly. Let stand until the icing sets, about 1 hour.

Serve immediately, or cover with a cake dome and store at room temperature for up to 1 day.

Makes one 10-inch (25-cm) cake; serves 12

Carrot Cake

2 cups (10 oz/315 g) unbleached
  all-purpose (plain) flour

2 teaspoons baking soda (bicarbonate
  of soda)

2 teaspoons baking powder

2 teaspoons ground cinnamon

½ teaspoon salt

½ teaspoon ground allspice

4 large eggs

¾ cup (6 fl oz/180 ml) vegetable oil

¾ cup (6 oz/185 g) granulated sugar

1 cup (7 oz/220 g) firmly packed
  brown sugar

½ cup (4 fl oz/125 ml) buttermilk

3 cups (12 oz/375 g) lightly packed
  peeled, shredded carrots

cream cheese frosting (recipe on page 14)

To save time in preparation, use a food processor fitted with the shredding disk to shred the carrots. This cake is also good flavored with coconut: Spread with coconut-flavored cream cheese frosting (recipe on page 14), then press 1 cup (3 oz/90 g) toasted sweetened shredded coconut evenly onto the sides of the cake for a decorative, flavorful finish.

*P*osition a rack in the middle of an oven and preheat to 350°F (180°C). Butter and flour 2 round cake pans each 9 inches (23 cm) in diameter and 2 inches (5 cm) deep.

In a medium bowl, sift together the flour, baking soda, baking powder, cinnamon, salt and allspice. In a large bowl, whisk together the eggs, vegetable oil, granulated sugar, brown sugar and buttermilk until blended.

Stir the flour mixture into the egg mixture just until combined. Fold in the carrots. Divide the batter evenly between the prepared pans.

Bake until a toothpick inserted into the centers comes out clean, about 40 minutes. Transfer to racks and let cool in the pans for 15 minutes. Invert the cakes onto the racks and let cool completely.

Place 1 cake layer on a plate. Spread 1¼ cups (10 fl oz/ 310 ml) of the frosting over the top. Place the second cake layer on top. Spread the remaining frosting decoratively over the top and sides of the cake. Serve immediately, or cover with a cake dome and refrigerate for up to 2 days. Bring to room temperature before serving.

Makes one 9-inch (23-cm) cake; serves 12

Hawaiian Upside-Down Cake

¼ cup (2 oz/60 g) unsalted butter, plus
  ½ cup (4 oz/125 g) unsalted butter,
  at room temperature

1¼ cups (9½ oz/295 g) firmly packed
  dark brown sugar

1 small ripe pineapple, about 3½ lb
  (1.75 kg), peeled, halved lengthwise,
  cored and cut into slices ½–¾ inch
  (12 mm–2 cm) thick

1 jar (7 oz/220 g) lightly salted or
  unsalted whole macadamia nuts
  (about 1½ cups)

1⅔ cups (8 oz/250 g) unbleached
  all-purpose (plain) flour

1 teaspoon baking powder

1 teaspoon baking soda (bicarbonate
  of soda)

¼ teaspoon salt

3 large eggs, at room temperature

1 teaspoon vanilla extract (essence)

2 tablespoons finely chopped
  crystallized ginger

⅔ cup (5 fl oz/160 ml) buttermilk

To dress up this homey and satisfying dessert, serve it with a scoop of vanilla ice cream drizzled with caramel sauce. If you like, replace the macadamias with whole blanched almonds.

Position a rack in the middle of an oven and preheat to 350°F (180°C).

In a 10-inch (25-cm) cast-iron frying pan over medium heat, melt together the ¼ cup (2 oz/60 g) butter and ¾ cup (6 oz/185 g) of the brown sugar. Remove from the heat and arrange enough of the pineapple slices atop the butter-sugar mixture in the bottom of the frying pan to cover decoratively. Fill the spaces with the macadamia nuts. Sprinkle any additional nuts over the pineapple slices.

In a bowl, sift together the flour, baking powder, baking soda and salt. In a large bowl, using an electric mixer set on medium speed, beat the ½ cup (4 oz/125 g) butter until light. Add the remaining ½ cup (3½ oz/110 g) brown sugar and beat until fluffy, about 2 minutes. Add the eggs, one at a time, beating well after each addition. Beat in the vanilla extract and then the ginger until well blended. Reduce the speed to low and, dividing the flour mixture into 3 batches, beat the flour mixture into the butter mixture alternately with the buttermilk, beginning and ending with the flour mixture. Spoon the batter evenly over the pineapple, spreading to cover completely.

Bake until a toothpick inserted into the center of the cake comes out clean, about 40 minutes. Let cool for 5 minutes.

Invert a platter over the frying pan. Wearing oven mitts, firmly grasp the platter and the pan together and invert them. Lift off the frying pan. Serve the cake warm.

Makes one 10-inch (25-cm) cake; serves 10

Applesauce-Spice Cake

1 cup (4 oz/125 g) plus 2 tablespoons
    pecan pieces

3⅓ cups (13½ oz/420 g) cake
    (soft-wheat) flour

1 tablespoon ground cinnamon

1½ teaspoons baking soda (bicarbonate
    of soda)

1¼ teaspoons ground allspice

1¼ teaspoons ground nutmeg

¼ teaspoon salt

1 cup (8 oz/250 g) unsalted butter,
    at room temperature

1⅔ cups (12 oz/375 g) firmly packed
    dark brown sugar

3 large eggs, at room temperature

2 teaspoons vanilla extract (essence)

2 cups (16 oz/500 g) unsweetened
    applesauce

confectioners' sugar icing flavored with
    brown sugar (*recipe on page 14*)

Applesauce gives this cake a marvelously moist texture. Use any plain, smooth unsweetened good-quality applesauce. For added spice, sprinkle some whipped cream with cinnamon and serve alongside.

Position a rack in the middle of an oven and preheat to 350°F (180°C). Spread the pecans on a baking sheet and place in the oven until lightly toasted, about 10 minutes. Set aside.

Leave the oven set at 350°F (180°C). Butter a 2½-qt (2½-l) nonstick bundt pan 10 inches (25 cm) in diameter and 3 inches (7.5 cm) deep.

In a medium bowl, sift together the flour, cinnamon, baking soda, allspice, nutmeg and salt. In a large bowl, using an electric mixer set on medium speed, beat together the butter and brown sugar until well blended. Add the eggs, one at a time, beating well after each addition. Beat in the vanilla extract. Dividing the flour mixture into 3 batches and using a wooden spoon, stir the flour mixture into the batter alternately with the applesauce, beginning and ending with the flour mixture. Stir in 1 cup (4 oz/125 g) of the toasted pecans. Spoon into the prepared pan.

Bake until a toothpick inserted near the center comes out clean, about 55 minutes. Transfer to a rack and let cool in the pan for 10 minutes. Invert onto the rack, turn right-side up and let cool completely.

Place the cake on a plate and drizzle the icing evenly over the top, allowing it to run over the sides slightly. Sprinkle on the remaining 2 tablespoons toasted pecans, then let stand until the icing sets, about 1 hour. Serve immediately, or cover with a cake dome and store at room temperature for up to 1 day.

Makes one 10-inch (25-cm) cake; serves 12

Mississippi Mud Cake

2 cups (10 oz/315 g) unbleached
  all purpose (plain) flour
2½ cups (1¼ lb/625 g) sugar
1 teaspoon baking soda (bicarbonate
  of soda)
½ teaspoon salt
1 cup (8 oz/250 g) unsalted butter
1½ cups (12 fl oz/375 ml) milk
¾ cup (2½ oz/75 g) unsweetened cocoa
2 large eggs, at room temperature
2 teaspoons vanilla extract (essence)
1½ cups (6 oz/185 g) pecan halves
bittersweet chocolate glaze (*recipe on*
  page 15)

This moist, delicious chocolate sheet cake fancifully takes its name from the dark, muddy Mississippi River. Take it in its pan to a picnic or family gathering. It's always a crowd pleaser. Walnut halves can be used in place of the pecans.

Position a rack in the middle of an oven and preheat to 350°F (180°C). Butter and flour a 15½-by-10½-by-1-inch (38.5-by-26-by-2.5-cm) jelly-roll pan.

Sift the flour into a large bowl. Add the sugar, baking soda and salt and stir to combine.

In a heavy saucepan over medium-high heat, combine the butter, milk and cocoa. Bring to a boil, whisking frequently until the butter melts. Add the cocoa mixture to the flour mixture, whisking until combined. Add the eggs and vanilla extract and whisk until well blended. Pour the batter into the prepared pan.

Bake until a toothpick inserted into the center comes out clean, about 15 minutes. Transfer to a rack and let cool completely in the pan.

Meanwhile, leave the oven set at 350°F (180°C). Spread the pecan halves on a baking sheet and place in the oven until toasted and fragrant, about 10 minutes. Let cool.

Arrange the toasted pecans evenly over the top of the cake. Then spoon the glaze over the top, covering completely. Let stand at room temperature until the glaze sets, about 3 hours.

Cut into squares and serve, or cover with aluminum foil and store for up to 2 days at room temperature.

Makes one 15½-by-10½-inch (38.5-by-26-cm) cake; serves 16–20

Sour Cream–Blueberry Cake

3 cups (15 oz/470 g) unbleached
  all-purpose (plain) flour
1 tablespoon baking powder
½ teaspoon salt
6 tablespoons (3 oz/90 g) unsalted
  butter, at room temperature
1⅓ cups (11 oz/340 g) sugar
2 large eggs
2 teaspoons vanilla extract (essence)
1 teaspoon grated lemon zest
¼ cup (2 fl oz/60 ml) sour cream
¾ cup (6 fl oz/180 ml) milk
2 cups (8 oz/250 g) fresh or frozen
  blueberries
confectioners' sugar icing flavored with
  lemon (recipe on page 14)

A terrific cake for brunch or afternoon tea. Look for fresh blueberries in the market during the warm summer months. Lime- or orange-flavored icing can replace the lemon icing (see page 14).

Position a rack in the middle of an oven and preheat to 350°F (180°C). Butter a 2½-qt (2.5-l) nonstick or regular bundt pan 10 inches (25 cm) in diameter and 3 inches (7.5 cm) deep.

In a medium bowl, sift together the flour, baking powder and salt. In a large bowl, using an electric mixer set on medium-high speed, beat the butter until light. Add the sugar and beat until blended. Add the eggs, one at a time, beating well after each addition. Beat in the vanilla extract and lemon zest and then the sour cream. Reduce the speed to low and, dividing the flour mixture into 3 batches, beat the flour mixture into the butter mixture alternately with the milk, beginning and ending with the flour mixture. Beat just until combined. The batter will be very thick.

Spoon half of the batter into the prepared pan. Sprinkle with 1 cup (4 oz/125 g) of the blueberries. Gently press the berries into the batter. Spoon the remaining batter over the berries and then sprinkle the remaining berries over the top, again pressing them gently into the batter.

Bake until a toothpick inserted near the center comes out clean, about 1 hour. Transfer to a rack and let cool in the pan for 10 minutes. Invert onto the rack and let cool completely.

Transfer the cake to a plate. Drizzle the icing evenly over the top, allowing it to run over the sides slightly. Serve immediately, or cover with a cake dome and store at room temperature for up to 1 day.

Makes one 10-inch (25-cm) cake; serves 10

Lime Angel Food Cake

1 cup (4 oz/125 g) cake (soft-wheat)
  flour
1 cup (4 oz/125 g) confectioners'
  (icing) sugar
1½ cups (12 fl oz/375 ml) egg whites
  (about 12 large), at room
  temperature
2 tablespoons fresh lime juice
1 teaspoon grated lime zest
1 teaspoon cream of tartar
¼ teaspoon salt
1 cup (8 oz/250 g) granulated sugar
confectioners' sugar icing flavored with
  lime (recipe on page 14)

As an angel food cake is cooled upside down, you will need either a tube pan with legs on the rim or a tube higher than the sides on which the pan can be balanced. If your tube pan has neither legs nor a tall tube, place the tube over the neck of a bottle to keep the cake elevated. If you like, just before serving, decorate the iced cake with pesticide-free edible flowers, such as pansies, nasturtiums or roses.

Position a rack in the middle of an oven and preheat to 350°F (180°C).

In a medium bowl, sift together the flour and confectioners' sugar. Resift the flour mixture twice. Set aside.

In a large bowl, using an electric mixer set on medium-high speed, beat together the egg whites; lime juice, lime zest, cream of tartar and salt until soft peaks form. Gradually add the granulated sugar, 2 tablespoons at a time, and continue beating until stiff, glossy peaks form. Sift one-fourth of the flour mixture over the egg white mixture. Using a rubber spatula, gently fold the flour mixture into the egg white mixture. Repeat the sifting and folding with the remaining flour mixture in 3 more batches. Spoon the batter into a nonstick or regular tube pan 9½ inches (24 cm) in diameter and 4 inches (10 cm) deep.

Bake until the cake springs back when lightly touched, about 45 minutes. Invert the cake in the pan onto a work surface (see note) and let cool completely.

When cool, run a sharp knife around the pan sides to loosen the cake and turn out of the pan. Place right-side up on a serving plate. Drizzle the icing over the top, allowing it to run over the sides slightly. Let stand until the icing sets, about 1 hour. Serve immediately, or cover with a cake dome and store at room temperature for up to 1 day.

Makes one 9½-inch (24-cm) cake; serves 8

Peaches-and-Cream "Shortcake"

1 vanilla bean, cut in half lengthwise

2 cans (12 fl oz/375 ml each) peach
   nectar

¼ cup (2 oz/60 g) granulated sugar

¼ cup (2 oz/60 g) unsalted butter,
   chilled, cut into tablespoon-sized
   pieces

1 cup (8 fl oz/250 ml) heavy (double)
   cream, chilled

½ cup (4 fl oz/125 ml) sour cream

2 tablespoons firmly packed dark
   brown sugar

butter pound cake, homemade (recipe
   on page 12) or store-bought

3 large ripe peaches, peeled, halved,
   pitted and sliced

*Pound cake is an excellent alternative to traditional shortcake
biscuits for making this old-fashioned American dessert. Polenta–
vanilla bean cake (recipe on page 17) would also make a delicious
base for the peaches and cream.*

Using a small sharp knife, scrape out the seeds from the vanilla
bean into a large, deep, heavy saucepan. Add the peach nectar
and granulated sugar and place over high heat. Bring to a
simmer. Reduce the heat to low and simmer, uncovered, until
reduced to 1½ cups (12 fl oz/375 ml), about 55 minutes.
Remove from the heat and whisk in the butter until melted. Let
cool completely.

In a large bowl, combine the heavy cream, sour cream and
brown sugar. Using an electric mixer set on medium-high
speed, beat until soft peaks form. Cover and refrigerate until
ready to use or for up to 8 hours.

Cut the cake into 12 slices, each about ½ inch (12 mm) thick.
Overlap 2 slices on each individual plate. Top each serving with
the peaches and then the cooled sauce, dividing it evenly.
Spoon a dollop of the whipped cream atop each serving. Serve
at once.

Serves 6

Hazelnut and Date Panforte

1¼ cups (6½ oz/200 g) hazelnuts
(filberts), lightly toasted (*see glossary,
page 106*) and cooled

⅓ cup (2 oz/60 g) all-purpose (plain)
flour

⅓ cup (1 oz/30 g) unsweetened cocoa,
plus extra for dusting

¾ teaspoon ground cinnamon

½ teaspoon ground nutmeg

¼ teaspoon ground cloves

¾ cup (4 oz/125 g) packed coarsely
chopped dried figs

¾ cup (4 oz/125 g) packed coarsely
chopped pitted dates

½ cup (3 oz/90 g) diced candied
orange peel or candied pineapple

1 tablespoon grated orange zest

½ cup (4 oz/125 g) plus 2 tablespoons
sugar

½ cup (6 oz/185 g) honey

¼ cup (2 fl oz/60 ml) fresh orange juice

2 tablespoons unsalted butter

8 oz (250 g) bittersweet chocolate,
chopped

*If you prefer a candylike texture, serve this Italian specialty chilled.
To store, wrap airtight and refrigerate for up to 1 month.*

*P*osition a rack in the middle of an oven and preheat to 300°F
(150°C). Butter a round cake pan 8 inches (20 cm) in diameter
and 2 inches (5 cm) deep. Line the bottom with parchment
paper cut to fit precisely. Generously butter the parchment paper.

In a large bowl, stir together the toasted hazelnuts, flour, the
⅓ cup (1 oz/30 g) cocoa, cinnamon, nutmeg, cloves, figs, dates,
candied orange peel or pineapple and orange zest. In a heavy
saucepan over medium heat, stir together the sugar, honey,
orange juice and butter. Heat, stirring, until the sugar dissolves,
about 3 minutes. Increase the heat to medium-high. Boil
without stirring until a candy thermometer registers 250°F
(120°C), about 5 minutes. Remove from the heat and stir in the
fruit mixture with a wooden spoon. Transfer the mixture to the
prepared pan, pushing it to the sides with the spoon.

Bake until the top feels dry, about 50 minutes. Transfer to a
rack and let cool in the pan for 10 minutes. Invert onto a baking
sheet; peel off the parchment. Let cool completely.

Place the chocolate in the top pan of a double boiler or in a
heatproof bowl. Set over (not touching) simmering water. Stir
until smooth and melted. Pour half of the chocolate over the top
of the cake; smooth with an icing spatula. Refrigerate until set,
about 1 hour.

Turn the cake over. Reheat the remaining chocolate over
simmering water just until warm; pour over the cake. Using the
spatula, spread to cover the top and sides. Refrigerate for 1 hour.

Using a fine-mesh sieve, sift enough cocoa over both sides of
the cake to cover lightly. Cut into wedges to serve.

Makes one 8-inch (20-cm) cake; serves 12

Fresh Strawberry–Vanilla Layer Cake

¼ cup (1 oz/30 g) confectioners' (icing) sugar

2 tablespoons strawberry preserves

1 tablespoon fresh lemon juice

2 cups (8 oz/250 g) thinly sliced, stemmed strawberries, plus 12–15 large strawberries with green leafy hulls intact, cut in half lengthwise through the hulls

¾ cup (3 oz/90 g) sliced almonds

butter pound cake, homemade (recipe on page 12) or store-bought

vanilla buttercream flavored with vanilla bean (recipe on page 13)

Perfect for a bridal shower or garden party. Select large, richly colored, blemish-free strawberries for decorating the top.

In a bowl, stir together the sugar, preserves and lemon juice. Add the sliced strawberries and toss gently. Let stand for 30 minutes.

Meanwhile, position a rack in the middle of an oven and preheat to 350°F (180°C). Spread the almonds on a baking sheet and place in the oven until toasted and fragrant, about 8 minutes. Let cool.

Using a long serrated knife, trim off the ends of the cake to make even surfaces. Turn the cake onto a long side and cut lengthwise into 6 long slices. Places 2 slices side by side on a platter to form a square. Drain the berries, reserving the juices. Brush the slices with half of the berry juices. Spread ½ cup (4 fl oz/125 ml) of the buttercream over the juice-soaked slices. Top with half of the sliced berries, arranging them in a single layer. Cover with 2 more cake slices, side by side. Brush these cake slices with the remaining berry juices and then spread another ½ cup (4 fl oz/125 ml) of the buttercream over them. Top with the remaining sliced berries, arranging them in a single layer. Top with the remaining cake slices, side by side.

Spread the remaining buttercream over the top and sides of the cake. Press the toasted almonds onto the sides of the cake. Arrange the halved berries in slightly overlapping rows atop the cake. Serve immediately, or cover with a cake dome and refrigerate for up to 1 day. Bring to room temperature before serving.

Makes one 8-inch (20-cm) square cake; serves 9

Chocolate Layer Cake

1¼ cups (6½ oz/200 g) unbleached
  all-purpose (plain) flour
½ cup (1½ oz/45 g) unsweetened cocoa
½ teaspoon salt
½ teaspoon baking powder
½ teaspoon baking soda (bicarbonate
  of soda)
¾ cup (6 oz/185 g) unsalted butter,
  at room temperature
1¼ cups (9 oz/280 g) firmly packed
  golden brown sugar
3 large eggs, at room temperature
⅔ cup (5 fl oz/160 ml) sour cream
sour cream fudge frosting (recipe on
  page 15)

A glass of ice-cold milk mates perfectly with this old-fashioned cake. For a special touch and extra flavor, press chopped toasted walnuts onto the sides of the frosted cake.

*P*osition a rack in the middle of an oven and preheat to 350°F (180°C). Butter 2 round cake pans each 9 inches (23 cm) in diameter and 2 inches (5 cm) deep. Line the bottom of each pan with parchment paper cut to fit precisely. Butter the paper.

In a small bowl, sift together the flour, cocoa, salt, baking powder and baking soda. In a large bowl, using an electric mixer set on medium-high speed, beat the butter until light. Gradually add the brown sugar, beating until fluffy, about 2 minutes. Add the eggs, one at a time, beating well after each addition. Reduce the speed to low and, dividing the flour mixture into 3 batches, beat the flour mixture into the butter mixture, alternately with the sour cream, beginning and ending with the flour mixture. The batter will be thick. Divide the batter between the prepared pans and smooth the tops with a rubber spatula.

Bake until a toothpick inserted into the centers comes out clean, about 25 minutes. Transfer to racks and let cool in the pans for 10 minutes. Invert the cakes onto the racks and peel off the parchment paper. Turn right-side up and let cool completely.

Place 1 cake layer on a plate. Spread ⅔ cup (5 fl oz/150 ml) of the frosting over the top. Place the second cake layer on top. Spread the remaining frosting over the top and sides of the cake. Using the back of a spoon, make a scallop pattern in the frosting all over the cake. Serve immediately, or cover with a cake dome and store at room temperature for up to 1 day.

Makes one 9-inch (23-cm) cake; serves 10

Poppyseed-Almond Cake

1¼ cups (10 oz/315 g) granulated sugar
⅓ cup (3 fl oz/80 ml) canola oil
2 large eggs, at room temperature
2 tablespoons poppyseeds
¾ teaspoon almond extract (essence)
1½ cups (6 oz/185 g) cake (soft-wheat)
  flour
¾ teaspoon baking powder
¼ teaspoon salt
½ cup (4 fl oz/125 ml) milk
⅓ cup (1½ oz/45 g) sliced almonds
confectioners' (icing) sugar

This moist, tender cake is great for a mid-morning treat. It can be stored in a lock-top plastic bag at room temperature for up to 2 days.

*P*osition a rack in the middle of an oven and preheat to 350°F (180°C). Butter and flour an 8½-by-4½-by-2½-inch (21-by-11-by-6-cm) loaf pan (6-cup/48-fl oz/1.5-l capacity).

In a large bowl, whisk together the granulated sugar, canola oil, eggs, poppyseeds and almond extract until blended. In a medium bowl, sift together the flour, baking powder and salt. Dividing the flour mixture into 3 batches, whisk the flour mixture into the egg mixture alternately with the milk, beginning and ending with the flour mixture. Pour the batter into the prepared pan. Sprinkle the almonds evenly over the top.

Bake until the top is deep brown and a toothpick inserted into the center comes out clean, about 1¼ hours. Transfer to a rack and let cool in the pan for 10 minutes. Invert onto the rack, turn right-side up and let cool completely.

Using a fine-mesh sieve, sift confectioners' sugar evenly over the top just before serving.

Makes 1 loaf cake; serves 8

Banana-Walnut Cake

¾ cup (3 oz/90 g) walnuts

1½ cups (7½ oz/235 g) unbleached
   all-purpose (plain) flour

¾ cup (6 oz/185 g) granulated sugar

1½ teaspoons baking soda (bicarbonate
   of soda)

¼ teaspoon salt

1¼ cups (10 oz/315 g) mashed very
   ripe banana (about 3 bananas)

½ cup (4 oz/125 g) unsalted butter,
   melted

1 large egg, at room temperature

3 tablespoons buttermilk

confectioners' (icing) sugar

*Serve this easy-to-make treat without frosting for a quick yet
delicious snack, or dress up the plain cake with vanilla buttercream (recipe on page 13) for a more sophisticated dessert.
Pecans or macadamia nuts can be substituted for the walnuts.*

Position a rack in the middle of an oven and preheat to
350°F (180°C). Spread the walnuts on a baking sheet and
place in the oven until lightly toasted and fragrant, about
10 minutes. Let cool and chop coarsely; set aside.

Leave the oven set at 350°F (180°C). Butter and flour an
8-inch (20-cm) square baking pan with 2-inch (5-cm) sides.

In a medium bowl, sift together the flour, granulated
sugar, baking soda and salt. In a large bowl, whisk together
the mashed banana, melted butter, egg and buttermilk
until well blended. Add the flour mixture to the banana
mixture and whisk just until combined. Stir in the toasted
walnuts. Transfer to the prepared pan and smooth the top
with a rubber spatula.

Bake until a toothpick inserted into the center comes out
clean, about 25 minutes. Transfer to a rack and let cool in
the pan until slightly warm or completely cool. Using a
fine-mesh sieve, sift confectioners' sugar evenly over the
top of the cake just before serving, then cut into 9 squares.
Using a metal spatula, remove the squares and serve warm
or at room temperature. The squares can be stored in an
airtight container at room temperature for up to 2 days.

Makes one 8-inch (20-cm) square cake; serves 9

Lemon Clove Tea Cake

1½ cups (6 oz/185 g) cake (soft-wheat) flour

1 teaspoon baking powder

¼ teaspoon salt

¼ teaspoon ground cloves

¾ cup (6 oz/185 g) unsalted butter, at room temperature

¾ cup (6 oz/185 g) granulated sugar

3 large eggs, at room temperature

1 tablespoon grated lemon zest

½ cup (2 oz/60 g) confectioners' (icing) sugar

3 tablespoons fresh lemon juice

Offer this dense lemon cake with a cup of hot tea or coffee. It is best served the day it is made. To store until serving, wrap in aluminum foil and keep at room temperature for up to 8 hours.

Position a rack in the middle of an oven and preheat to 350°F (180°C). Butter and flour an 8½-by-4½-by-2½-inch (21-by-11-by-6-cm) loaf pan (6-cup/48-fl oz/1.5-l capacity).

In a medium bowl, sift together the flour, baking powder, salt and cloves. Set aside. In a large bowl, using an electric mixer set on medium-high speed, beat the butter until light. Gradually add the granulated sugar, beating until fluffy and ivory colored, about 2 minutes.

In a small bowl, whisk together the eggs and lemon zest until blended. Using the electric mixer set on medium speed, gradually beat the egg mixture into the butter mixture. Reduce the speed to low and beat in the flour mixture just until combined. Transfer the batter to the prepared pan; smooth the top with a rubber spatula.

Bake until a toothpick inserted into the center comes out clean, about 1 hour. Transfer to a rack; let cool in the pan for 5 minutes. Invert onto the rack and turn right-side up.

In a small bowl, whisk together the confectioners' sugar and lemon juice until blended. Brush the mixture over the top and sides of the hot cake. Let cool completely before serving.

Makes 1 loaf cake; serves 8

Warm Pear Cake with Walnut Caramel Topping

1 cup (4 oz/125 g) walnuts

1 cup (5 oz/155 g) unbleached
all-purpose (plain) flour

½ teaspoon ground cinnamon

½ teaspoon baking soda (bicarbonate
of soda)

¼ teaspoon ground nutmeg

¼ teaspoon salt

1 cup (7 oz/220 g) firmly packed
golden brown sugar

5 tablespoons (2½ oz/75 g) unsalted
butter, melted, plus ¼ cup
(2 oz/60 g) unsalted butter

2 large eggs, at room temperature

¼ cup (2 fl oz/60 ml) pear nectar

1 ripe pear, peeled, cored and cut into
½-inch (12-mm) cubes (about 1 cup/
6 oz/185 g)

1 tablespoon milk

*Macadamias or hazelnuts (filberts) are also good choices for this
cake. It is best served warm from the oven, but it can be allowed to
cool completely in its pan, covered with aluminum foil and stored at
room temperature for up to 8 hours. To reheat, place in a 350°F
(180°C) oven for 10 minutes. Serve with vanilla ice cream, if you like.*

*P*osition a rack in the middle of an oven and preheat to 350°F
(180°C). Spread the walnuts on a baking sheet and place in the
oven until lightly toasted and fragrant, about 10 minutes. Let
cool and chop coarsely; set aside.

Leave the oven set at 350°F (180°C). Butter and flour a 9-inch
(23-cm) springform pan with 2-inch (5-cm) sides.

In a medium bowl, sift together the flour, cinnamon, baking
soda, nutmeg and salt. In a large bowl, using an electric mixer
set on medium speed, beat together ¾ cup (5½ oz/170 g) of the
brown sugar, the 5 tablespoons melted butter, eggs and nectar
until blended. Stir in the flour mixture just until combined and
then the pear cubes. Transfer the batter to the prepared pan.

Bake until a toothpick inserted into the center comes out
clean, about 25 minutes. Transfer the pan to a rack.

In a medium-sized, heavy saucepan over medium-high heat,
combine the toasted walnuts, the remaining ¼ cup (1½ oz/50 g)
brown sugar, the ¼ cup (2 oz/60 g) butter and the milk. Bring
to a boil, stirring frequently, and then boil, stirring frequently,
until the mixture is reduced to a thick sauce consistency, about
3 minutes. Pour the hot nut mixture over the hot cake in the
pan. Let stand for 3 minutes.

Release the pan sides and place the cake on a plate. Cut into
wedges and serve warm.

Makes one 9-inch (23-cm) cake; serves 6

Almond Roca Cake

butter pound cake, homemade *(recipe on page 12)* or store-bought
sour cream fudge frosting flavored with mocha *(recipe on page 15)*
½ cup (2½ oz/75 g) plus 1 tablespoon finely chopped Almond Roca toffee candy or Heath bars

If time is limited, purchase pound cake from a bakery or food store to make assembling this cake even easier. Any hard chocolate-covered toffee candy can be used in place of the Almond Roca or Heath bars.

Using a long serrated knife, cut the pound cake horizontally into 4 layers. Place the bottom cake layer cut-side up on a plate. Spread ¼ cup (2 fl oz/60 ml) of the frosting over the layer. Sprinkle with 2 tablespoons of the chopped toffee. Spread the underside of the second cake layer with 1 tablespoon of the frosting and place frosting-side down atop the toffee-covered layer. Spread ¼ cup (2 fl oz/60 ml) of the frosting over the second cake layer. Sprinkle with 2 tablespoons of the toffee. Spread the underside of the third cake layer with 1 tablespoon frosting and again place frosting-side down atop the toffee-covered layer. Spread ¼ cup (2 fl oz/60 ml) of the frosting over the third cake layer. Sprinkle with 2 tablespoons of the toffee.

Now spread the underside of the fourth cake layer with 1 tablespoon frosting and place frosted-side down atop the cake. Spread the remaining frosting over the top and sides of the cake. Sprinkle the top edges of the cake with the remaining 3 tablespoons chopped toffee. Let stand until the frosting sets slightly, about 1 hour.

Serve immediately, or cover with a cake dome and store at room temperature for up to 1 day.

Makes 1 loaf cake; serves 10

Fig, Hazelnut and Anise Cake

⅔ cup (3½ oz/105 g) hazelnuts
  (filberts)
1½ cups (7½ oz/235 g) unbleached
  all-purpose (plain) flour
1 teaspoon baking powder
½ teaspoon ground nutmeg
1½ cups (8 oz/250 g) chopped dried
  figs
¾ cup (6 oz/185 g) unsalted butter,
  at room temperature
⅔ cup (5 oz/155 g) granulated sugar
3 large eggs, at room temperature
2 teaspoons grated orange zest
½ teaspoon anise extract (essence)
confectioners' sugar icing flavored with
  orange (recipe on page 14)

Offer this dense fruit-and-nut-filled cake as part of an afternoon tea. It is best eaten the same day it is made.

Position a rack in the middle of an oven and preheat to 350°F (180°C). Spread the hazelnuts on a baking sheet and place in the oven until lightly toasted and fragrant, about 10 minutes. Let cool and chop coarsely; set aside.

Leave the oven set at 350°F (180°C). Butter and flour an 8½-by-4½-by-2½-inch (21-by-11-by-6-cm) loaf pan (6-cup/48-fl oz/1.5-l capacity).

In a large bowl, sift together the flour, baking powder and nutmeg. Add the figs and hazelnuts and toss to coat with the dry ingredients. In another large bowl, using an electric mixer set on medium-high speed, beat the butter until light. Gradually add the sugar, beating until fluffy and ivory colored, about 2 minutes. Add the eggs, one at a time, beating well after each addition. Beat in the orange zest and anise extract. Stir in the flour mixture. The mixture will be very stiff and resemble soft cookie dough. Spoon the mixture into the prepared pan.

Bake until a toothpick inserted into the center comes out clean, about 1¼ hours. Transfer to a rack and let cool in the pan for 10 minutes. Invert onto the rack, turn right-side up and let cool completely.

Place the cake on a plate and drizzle the icing evenly over the top, allowing it to run over the sides slightly. Let stand until the icing sets, about 1 hour, then serve.

Makes 1 loaf cake; serves 8

Pistachio-Apricot Cake

2⅔ cups (11½ oz/360 g) shelled unsalted pistachio nuts

1⅔ cups (13 oz/400 g) sugar

½ cup (2½ oz/75 g) unbleached all-purpose (plain) flour

¼ teaspoon salt

6 large eggs, separated, at room temperature

5 tablespoons (2½ oz/75 g) unsalted butter, melted and kept warm

½ teaspoon cream of tartar

vanilla buttercream flavored with vanilla bean (recipe on page 13)

½ cup (5 oz/155 g) apricot preserves, melted

10 fresh apricots, pitted and sliced

*P*osition a rack in the middle of an oven and preheat to 350°F (180°C). Butter and flour a 15½-by-10½-by-1-inch (38.5-by-26-by-2.5-cm) jelly-roll pan. Line the bottom with parchment paper cut to fit precisely.

In a food processor fitted with the metal blade, combine 2 cups (8 oz/250 g) of the pistachios, ⅔ cup (5 oz/150 g) of the sugar, the flour and salt. Process to grind finely. Set aside. In a large bowl, whisk together well the egg yolks and the remaining 1 cup (8 oz/250 g) sugar. Whisk in the warm butter.

In a large bowl, using an electric mixer set on high speed, beat together the egg whites and cream of tartar until stiff peaks form. Using a rubber spatula, fold one-third of the nut mixture, then one-third of the beaten whites into the yolk mixture. Repeat this procedure twice using the remaining nuts and whites. Do not overmix. Transfer the batter to the prepared pan; smooth the top with the spatula.

Bake until a toothpick inserted into the center comes out clean, 28–30 minutes. Transfer to a rack and let cool.

Run a knife around the pan sides to loosen the cake. Invert onto a work surface; peel off the parchment. Cut the cake crosswise into 3 strips each about 10 by 5 inches (25 by 13 cm). Place 1 strip on a platter. Spread ⅓ cup (3 fl oz/80 ml) of the buttercream on top. Drizzle with half of the melted preserves. Place the second cake strip on top of the first. Spread ⅓ cup (3 fl oz/80 ml) of the buttercream on top. Drizzle with the remaining melted preserves. Place the third cake strip on top. Spread the remaining buttercream over the top and sides of the cake. Press the remaining ⅔ cup (3½ oz/110 g) nuts onto the sides. (To store the cake, cover with plastic wrap and refrigerate for up to 1 day. Bring to room temperature before continuing.) Arrange the apricot slices atop the cake and serve.

Makes one 10-by-5-inch (25-by-13-cm) cake; serves 12

Golden Cake with Tangerine Fudge Frosting

2 cups (10 oz/315 g) unbleached
  all-purpose (plain) flour
1 teaspoon baking powder
1 teaspoon baking soda (bicarbonate
  of soda)
½ teaspoon salt
½ cup (4 oz/125 g) unsalted butter,
  at room temperature
1½ cups (12 oz/375 g) sugar
2 teaspoons vanilla extract (essence)
4 large eggs plus 2 large egg yolks, at
  room temperature
1 cup (8 fl oz/250 ml) buttermilk
sour cream fudge frosting flavored with
  tangerine *(recipe on page 15)*

This simple cake, with its rich citrus-flavored fudge frosting, is perfect for taking along on a picnic, as it can be transported in its baking pan. If you like, garnish it with a sprinkling of tangerine or orange zest.

Position a rack in the middle of an oven and preheat to 350°F (180°C). Butter and flour a 13-by-9-by-2-inch (33-by-23-by-5-cm) metal baking pan.

In a medium bowl, sift together the flour, baking powder, baking soda and salt. In a large bowl, using an electric mixer set on medium-high speed, beat the butter until light. Gradually add the sugar, beating until well blended. Beat in the vanilla extract. Add the eggs and egg yolks, one at a time, beating well after each addition. Reduce the speed to low and, dividing the flour mixture into 3 batches, beat the flour mixture into the butter mixture alternately with the buttermilk, beginning and ending with the flour mixture. Once the mixtures are combined, continue to beat for 30 seconds. Transfer the batter to the prepared pan.

Bake until the top is a deep golden brown and a toothpick inserted into the center comes out clean, 35–40 minutes. Transfer to a rack and let cool completely in the pan.

Spread the frosting over the cake and cut into 12 squares. Serve immediately, or cover with aluminum foil and store at room temperature for up to 1 day.

Makes one 13-by-9-inch (33-by-23-cm) cake; serves 12

Walnut Dacquoise

⅔ cup (2½ oz/75 g) plus ½ cup
    (2 oz/60 g) walnuts, lightly toasted
    (see glossary, page 106) and cooled,
    plus 8 walnut halves
¾ cup (6 oz/180 g) sugar
1 tablespoon cornstarch
3 large egg whites, at room temperature
½ teaspoon cream of tartar
½ teaspoon vanilla extract (essence)
vanilla buttercream flavored with coffee
    (recipe on page 13)

*P*osition a rack in the middle of an oven and preheat to 250°F (120°C). Line the bottoms of 2 large baking sheets with parchment paper cut to fit precisely. Firmly trace one 8-inch (20-cm) circle on 1 sheet and two 8-inch (20-cm) circles on the second sheet. Turn the parchment sheets over; the traced circles should be visible.

In a food processor fitted with the metal blade, combine the ⅔ cup (2½ oz/75 g) toasted walnuts, ¼ cup (2 oz/60 g) of the sugar and the cornstarch. Process to grind the nuts finely. Set aside. In a large bowl, combine the egg whites and cream of tartar. Using an electric mixer set on medium-high speed, beat until soft peaks form. Gradually add the remaining ½ cup (4 oz/120 g) sugar, beating until stiff, glossy peaks form. Beat in the vanilla. Using a rubber spatula, gently fold in the nut mixture.

Divide the egg white mixture evenly among the traced circles. Using the back of a spoon, spread the mixture to fill the circles evenly. Bake until the outsides are crisp and pale gold, about 1 hour and 20 minutes. Transfer to a work surface and let cool on the baking sheets for 10 minutes. Then carefully peel the meringues off the parchment paper and let cool on racks.

Place 1 meringue on a platter. Spread ⅓ cup (3 fl oz/90 ml) of the buttercream over the top. Place a second meringue on top. Again spread with ⅓ cup (3 fl oz/90 ml) of the buttercream. Top with the third meringue. Then spread the remaining buttercream over the top and sides of the stacked layers. Finely chop the ½ cup (2 oz/60 g) walnuts. Press them onto the sides of the cake. Arrange the walnut halves around the top.

Refrigerate until the buttercream sets, about 1 hour. Then cover with plastic wrap and refrigerate overnight to allow the meringues to soften. Bring to room temperature before serving.

Makes one 8-inch (20-cm) cake; serves 8

Chocolate Cupcakes with Peppermint Fudge Frosting

1 cup (5 oz/155 g) unbleached
  all-purpose (plain) flour

1 cup (8 oz/250 g) plus 2 tablespoons
  sugar

½ teaspoon baking soda (bicarbonate
  of soda)

¼ teaspoon salt

¾ cup (6 fl oz/180 ml) milk

½ cup (4 oz/125 g) unsalted butter

⅓ cup (1⅓ oz/40 g) firmly packed
  unsweetened cocoa

1 large egg, at room temperature

1 teaspoon vanilla extract (essence)

sour cream fudge frosting flavored with
  peppermint (recipe on page 15)

2 tablespoons coarsely crushed red-
  and-white striped peppermint
  candies, optional

These treats would be especially appreciated at a children's party. If you choose to use the peppermint candies, don't crush them too far in advance, as they will become sticky when exposed to air. A small food processor works well for this step; or place the candies in a lock-top plastic bag and crush with the bottom of a heavy frying pan. For a double dose of chocolate without the mint accent, omit the candies and the peppermint extract in the frosting

*P*osition a rack in the middle of an oven and preheat to 350°F (180°C). Line ten ½-cup (4-fl oz/125-ml) muffin-pan cups with paper liners.

Sift the flour into a large bowl. Stir in the sugar, baking soda and salt. In a heavy saucepan over medium-high heat, combine the milk, butter and cocoa. Bring to a boil, whisking constantly. Remove from the heat and add to the flour mixture, whisking until well combined. Whisk in the egg and vanilla extract until blended. Spoon an equal amount of the batter into each prepared muffin cup.

Bake until a toothpick inserted into the center of a cupcake comes out clean, about 25 minutes. The cakes will be flat on top when they are baked. Remove from the oven and immediately invert onto a rack. Turn the cupcakes right-side up. Let cool completely.

Spread about 2 tablespoons frosting over each cupcake. (If you wish to store the cupcakes, pack in a single layer in an airtight container and refrigerate for up to 2 days. Bring to room temperature before serving.) Sprinkle with crushed peppermint candies before serving, if desired.

Makes 10 cupcakes

Sunshine Cupcakes

1⅓ cups (7 oz/220 g) unbleached
   all-purpose (plain) flour
1¼ teaspoons baking powder
½ teaspoon baking soda (bicarbonate
   of soda)
¼ teaspoon salt
¾ cup (6 oz/185 g) sugar
¼ cup (2 oz/60 g) unsalted butter
⅔ cup (5 fl oz/160 ml) milk
1½ teaspoons grated lemon zest
1½ teaspoons grated orange zest
1 large egg plus 1 large egg yolk, at
   room temperature
double recipe confectioners' sugar
   icing flavored with lemon
   (recipe on page 14)

These citrus-flavored cakes with lemon icing deliver a wonderful sweet-tart taste sensation. You can make standard-sized cupcakes or miniature cakes just a little bigger than a mouthful. In either case, you will need to make a double batch of the icing to frost all of the cakes.

Position a rack in the middle of an oven and preheat to 350°F (180°C). Line ten ½-cup (4-fl oz/125-ml) muffin-pan cups or 32 miniature 1½-tablespoon muffin-pan cups with paper liners.

In a large bowl, sift together the flour, baking powder, baking soda and salt. Mix in the sugar. In a small, heavy saucepan over medium heat, combine the butter, milk and lemon and orange zests and heat until the butter melts. Whisk the hot milk mixture into the flour mixture until well combined. Then add the whole egg and egg yolk and whisk until blended. Spoon about 3 tablespoons batter into each standard-sized muffin cup, or 1 level tablespoon batter into each mini muffin cup.

Bake until a toothpick inserted into the center of a cupcake comes out clean, about 20 minutes for standard cupcakes and 12 minutes for mini cupcakes. Remove from the oven and immediately invert onto a rack. Turn the cupcakes right-side up. Let cool completely. (If you wish to store the cupcakes, pack in an airtight container and keep at room temperature for up to 2 days before icing.)

Spread the icing over the cupcakes and serve.

Makes 10 standard or 32 miniature cupcakes

Pineapple Cupcakes with Coconut Buttercream

1 cup (4 oz/125 g) sweetened shredded
  coconut

1⅓ cups (7 oz/220 g) unbleached
  all-purpose (plain) flour

1¼ teaspoons baking powder

½ teaspoon baking soda (bicarbonate
  of soda)

¼ teaspoon salt

¼ cup (2 oz/60 g) unsalted butter,
  at room temperature

⅔ cup (5 oz/155 g) sugar

2 large eggs plus 1 large egg yolk, at
  room temperature

1 can (8 oz/250 g) unsweetened
  crushed pineapple, well drained

⅓ cup (3 fl oz/80 ml) pineapple juice

¾ cup (6 fl oz/180 ml) vanilla
  buttercream flavored with coconut
  (recipe on page 13)

The coconut buttercream and the toasted coconut topping give these light, moist cupcakes a wonderful tropical accent. You can also frost them with plain vanilla buttercream (recipe on page 13), if you like.

Position a rack in the middle of an oven and preheat to 350°F (180°C). Spread the coconut on a baking sheet and place in the oven until lightly toasted, about 8 minutes. Let cool.

Leave the oven set at 350°F (180°C). Line twelve ½-cup (4-fl oz/125-ml) muffin-pan cups with paper liners.

In a medium bowl, sift together the flour, baking powder, baking soda and salt. In a large bowl, using an electric mixer set on medium-high speed, beat the butter until light. Gradually add the sugar, beating until fluffy and ivory colored, about 2 minutes. Add the whole eggs and egg yolk, one at a time, beating well after each addition. Beat in the crushed pineapple. Reduce the speed to low and, dividing the flour mixture into 3 batches, beat the flour mixture into the butter mixture alternately with the pineapple juice, beginning and ending with the flour mixture. Beat just until blended. Spoon an equal amount of the batter into each prepared muffin cup.

Bake until a toothpick inserted in the center comes out clean, about 20 minutes. Remove from the oven and immediately invert onto a rack. Turn the cupcakes right-side up. Let cool.

Spread about 1 tablespoon buttercream over each cupcake. Sprinkle generously with the toasted coconut, covering completely, and serve. To store, pack in a single layer in an airtight container and refrigerate for up to 2 days. Bring to room temperature before serving.

Makes 12 cupcakes

Chocolate Chip–Banana Cupcakes

1½ cups (7½ oz/235 g) unbleached
   all-purpose (plain) flour

¾ cup (6 oz/185 g) sugar

1½ teaspoons baking soda (bicarbonate
   of soda)

¼ teaspoon salt

1¼ cups (10 oz/315 g) mashed very
   ripe banana (about 3 bananas)

½ cup (4 oz/125 g) unsalted butter,
   melted

1 large egg, at room temperature

3 tablespoons buttermilk

½ cup (3 oz/90 g) semisweet chocolate
   chips

about 1 cup (8 fl oz/250 ml) vanilla
   buttercream (*recipe on page 13*)

These moist treats marry two complementary flavors, banana and chocolate. For a double-chocolate treat, substitute sour cream fudge frosting (recipe on page 15) for the buttercream.

Position a rack in the middle of an oven and preheat to 350°F (180°C). Line fourteen ½-cup (4-fl oz/125-ml) muffin-pan cups with paper liners.

In a medium bowl, sift together the flour, sugar, baking soda and salt. In a large bowl, whisk together the mashed banana, melted butter, egg and buttermilk until well blended. Add the flour mixture and whisk just until combined. Stir in the chocolate chips. Spoon an equal amount of the batter into each prepared muffin cup.

Bake until a toothpick inserted into the center of a cupcake comes out clean, about 25 minutes. Remove from the oven and immediately invert onto a rack. Turn the cupcakes right-side up. Let cool completely.

To serve, spread about 1 tablespoon buttercream over each cupcake. To store, pack in a single layer in an airtight container and refrigerate for up to 2 days. Bring to room temperature before serving.

Makes 14 cupcakes

Raspberry Surprise Cupcakes

1½ cups (7½ oz/235 g) unbleached
    all-purpose (plain) flour

2 teaspoons baking powder

¼ teaspoon salt

1 cup (8 oz/250 g) sugar

¾ cup (6 fl oz/180 ml) milk

6 tablespoons (3 oz/90 g) unsalted
    butter, melted

3 large egg whites, at room temperature

1 teaspoon vanilla extract (essence)

3 tablespoons raspberry preserves

double recipe confectioners' sugar icing
    flavored with lemon (*recipe on page 14*)

These light cupcakes each carry a pocket of sweet raspberry preserves that is revealed when you bite into them. You can use lime or orange for flavoring the icing; or try your own favorite citrus-flavored icing.

Position a rack in the middle of an oven and preheat to 350°F (180°C). Line eleven ½-cup (4-fl oz/125-ml) muffin-pan cups with paper liners.

In a medium bowl, sift together the flour, baking powder and salt. Stir in the sugar. Add the milk, melted butter, egg whites and vanilla extract; whisk until smooth. Spoon an equal amount of the batter into each prepared muffin cup.

Bake until a toothpick inserted into the center of a cupcake comes out clean, about 20 minutes. Remove from the oven and immediately invert onto racks. Turn the cupcakes right-side up. Let cool completely. (If you wish to store the cupcakes, pack them into an airtight container and keep at room temperature for up to 2 days before filling and icing.)

Using the small end of a melon baller, cut out a pocket in the top center of each cupcake. Spoon ¾ teaspoon raspberry preserves into each pocket. Spread the icing over the cupcakes and serve.

Makes 11 cupcakes

Honey-Nectarine Cheesecake

FOR THE CRUST:

1 cup (4 oz/125 g) sliced almonds

1 cup (3 oz/90 g) graham cracker
crumbs

¼ cup (2 oz/60 g) firmly packed
brown sugar

5 tablespoons (2½ oz/75 g) unsalted
butter, melted and cooled

FOR THE FILLING:

2 lb (1 kg) cream cheese, at room
temperature

⅓ cup (4 oz/125 g) honey

¼ cup (2 oz/60 g) granulated sugar

1 cup (8 fl oz/250 ml) heavy (double)
cream

2 tablespoons fresh lemon juice

½ teaspoon almond extract (essence)

1 tablespoon water

1 teaspoon unflavored gelatin

3 tablespoons apricot or peach jam

4 ripe nectarines, halved, pitted and
sliced

Preheat an oven to 350°F (180°C). Spread the almonds on a
baking sheet and place in the oven until lightly toasted and
fragrant, about 10 minutes. Let cool.

Leave the oven set at 350°F (180°C). In a food processor fitted
with the metal blade, combine the toasted almonds, graham
cracker crumbs and brown sugar. Process to grind finely. Add
the melted butter and process until the crumbs begin to stick
together. With your hand draped with plastic wrap to form a
glove, press the crumbs firmly onto the bottom and 2 inches
(5 cm) up the sides of a springform pan 9 inches (23 cm) in
diameter and 2½ inches (6 cm) deep. Bake the crust for
10 minutes until set. Remove from the oven and let cool.

To make the filling, in a large bowl, combine the cream cheese,
honey and granulated sugar. Using an electric mixer set on
medium speed, beat until smooth and well blended. Beat in
½ cup (4 fl oz/125 ml) of the cream, the lemon juice and
almond extract until smooth.

Place the water in a small saucepan. Sprinkle the gelatin over
the top and let soften for 5 minutes. Place over low heat and stir
until the gelatin dissolves. Gradually whisk in the remaining
½ cup (4 fl oz/125 ml) cream. Then add the gelatin mixture to
the cream cheese mixture and beat until fluffy, about 1 minute.
Spoon the filling into the cooled crust. Cover with aluminum
foil and refrigerate overnight or for up to 2 days.

To serve, run a knife around the pan sides to loosen the cake.
Release the pan sides and place the cake on a plate.

In a small, heavy saucepan over medium heat, stir the apricot
or peach jam until melted. Remove from the heat and let cool
slightly. Arrange the nectarine slices atop the cake. Using a
pastry brush, brush the jam over the fruit, then cut into wedges.

Makes one 9-inch (23-cm) cake; serves 12

Pumpkin-Hazelnut Cheesecake

FOR THE CRUST:

2 cups (6 oz/185 g) gingersnap cookie crumbs

¼ cup (2 oz/60 g) firmly packed brown sugar

5 tablespoons (2½ oz/75 g) unsalted butter, melted and cooled

FOR THE FILLING:

2 lb (1 kg) cream cheese, at room temperature

1⅓ cups (9½ oz/295 g) firmly packed brown sugar

1⅓ cups (10½ oz/330 g) canned solid-pack pumpkin purée

1 tablespoon vanilla extract (essence)

1½ teaspoons ground cinnamon

¼ teaspoon ground allspice

5 large eggs, at room temperature

FOR THE TOPPING:

1 cup (5 oz/155 g) hazelnuts (filberts)

¼ cup (2 oz/60 g) firmly packed brown sugar

¼ cup (2 oz/60 g) unsalted butter

¼ cup (2 fl oz/60 ml) heavy (double) cream

*P*osition a rack in the middle of an oven and preheat to 350°F (180°C). To make the crust, in a food processor fitted with the metal blade, combine the gingersnap crumbs and brown sugar. Process to mix well. Add the melted butter and process until the crumbs begin to stick together. With your hand draped with plastic wrap to form a glove, press the crumbs firmly onto the bottom and 2 inches (5 cm) up the sides of a springform pan 9 inches (23 cm) in diameter and 2½ inches (6 cm) deep. Wrap aluminum foil around the outside of the pan. Bake the crust for 10 minutes until set. Remove from the oven and let cool. Leave the oven set at 350°F (180°C).

To make the filling, in a large bowl, combine the cream cheese and brown sugar. Using an electric mixer set on medium speed, beat until well blended. Beat in the pumpkin, vanilla, cinnamon and allspice. Add the eggs, one at a time, beating after each addition just until combined. Pour the filling into the cooled crust, spreading it to the edges of the pan.

Bake until the cheesecake puffs and the center is almost set, about 1½ hours. Transfer to a rack and let cool for 1 hour.

Meanwhile, make the topping: Leave the oven set at 350°F (180°C). Spread the hazelnuts on a baking sheet and place in the oven until lightly toasted, about 10 minutes. Set aside. In a small, heavy pan over medium heat, combine the brown sugar, butter and cream and stir until the sugar dissolves. Raise the heat and bring to a boil. Add the hazelnuts and boil, stirring occasionally, until the mixture thinly coats the nuts, about 2 minutes. Spoon evenly over the cooled cake and let cool. Cover with aluminum foil and refrigerate overnight or for up to 4 days.

To serve, run a knife around the pan sides to loosen the cake. Remove the foil from the pan and release the pan sides. Place the cheesecake on a plate and cut into wedges.

Makes one 9-inch (23-cm) cake; serves 12

Classic Lemon Cheesecake

FOR THE CRUST:

1¾ cups (5½ oz/170 g) graham cracker crumbs

¼ cup (2 oz/60 g) firmly packed brown sugar

1 teaspoon grated lemon zest

½ cup (4 oz/125 g) unsalted butter, melted and cooled

FOR THE FILLING:

2 lb (1 kg) cream cheese, at room temperature

1 cup (8 oz/250 g) granulated sugar

1 cup (8 fl oz/250 ml) heavy (double) cream

3 tablespoons fresh lemon juice

2 teaspoons grated lemon zest

1 tablespoon water

1 teaspoon unflavored gelatin

3 thin lemon slices

For a fancier dessert, top the cake with your favorite tropical fruits. Sliced peeled mango, papaya and pineapple are a winning trio. Once the cheesecake has been topped with fruit, it should be stored in the refrigerator for no more than 4 hours.

Preheat an oven to 350°F (180°C). To make the crust, in a food processor fitted with the metal blade, combine the graham cracker crumbs, brown sugar and lemon zest. Process to mix well. Add the butter and process until the crumbs begin to stick together. With your hand draped with plastic wrap to form a glove, press the crumbs firmly onto the bottom and 2 inches (5 cm) up the sides of a springform pan 9 inches (23 cm) in diameter and 2½ inches (6 cm) deep. Bake the crust for 10 minutes until set. Remove from the oven and let cool.

To make the filling, in a large bowl, combine the cream cheese and granulated sugar. Using an electric mixer set on medium speed, beat until well blended. Beat in ½ cup (4 fl oz/125 ml) of the cream, the lemon juice and lemon zest until incorporated.

Place the water in a small saucepan. Sprinkle the gelatin over the water and let soften for 5 minutes. Place the saucepan over low heat and stir until dissolved. Gradually whisk in the remaining ½ cup (4 fl oz/125 ml) cream. Then add the gelatin mixture to the cream cheese mixture and beat until fluffy, about 1 minute. Spoon the filling into the cooled crust. Cover with aluminum foil and refrigerate overnight or for up to 2 days.

To serve, run a knife around the pan sides to loosen the cake. Release the pan sides and place the cake on a plate. Overlap the lemon slices atop the center of the cake and cut into wedges.

Makes one 9-inch (23-cm) cake; serves 12

Coconut Cheesecake

FOR THE CRUST:

1 cup (4 oz/125 g) sweetened shredded
    coconut, toasted (see glossary, page 105)
1 cup (3 oz/90 g) graham cracker
    crumbs
¼ cup (2 oz/60 g) sugar
7 tablespoons (3½ oz/105 g) unsalted
    butter, melted and cooled

FOR THE FILLING:

2 lb (1 kg) cream cheese, at room
    temperature
¾ cup (6 oz/185 g) sugar
1 can (15 fl oz/470 ml) sweetened
    cream of coconut
2 tablespoons all purpose (plain) flour
4 large eggs, at room temperature
1 cup (4 oz/125 g) sweetened shredded
    coconut, toasted (see glossary, page 105)

FOR THE TOPPING:

1¼ cups (5 oz/155 g) sweetened
    shredded coconut, toasted
    (see glossary, page 105)
bittersweet chocolate glaze for topping
    cheesecake (recipe on page 15)

Position a rack in the middle of an oven and preheat to 350°F (180°C). To make the crust, in a food processor fitted with the metal blade, combine the toasted coconut, graham cracker crumbs, sugar and melted butter. Process until the crumbs begin to stick together. With your hand draped with plastic wrap to form a glove, press the crumb mixture firmly onto the bottom and 2 inches (5 cm) up the sides of a springform pan 9 inches (23 cm) in diameter and 2½ inches (6 cm) deep. Wrap aluminum foil around the outside of the pan. Bake the crust for 10 minutes until set. Remove from the oven and let cool. Leave the oven set at 350°F (180°C).

To make the filling, in a large bowl, combine the cream cheese and sugar. Using an electric mixer set on medium speed, beat until well blended. Beat in the cream of coconut and flour until combined. Add the eggs, one at a time, beating after each addition just until combined. Stir in the toasted coconut. Pour the filling into the cooled crust.

Bake until the top browns (it may crack around the edges) and quivers slightly all over when the cake is shaken, about 1 hour and 20 minutes. Transfer to a rack and let cool. Cover with aluminum foil and refrigerate overnight.

The next day, run a knife around the pan sides to loosen the cake. To top the cake, sprinkle with 1 cup (4 oz/125 g) of the toasted coconut. Spoon the lukewarm glaze over the coconut. Sprinkle the edges with the remaining ¼ cup (1 oz/30 g) coconut. Refrigerate until set, at least 2 hours. (To store the cake, cover with aluminum foil and refrigerate for up to 4 days.)

To serve, remove the foil from the pan and release the pan sides. Place the cheesecake on a plate and cut into wedges.

Makes one 9-inch (23-cm) cake; serves 12

Holiday Eggnog Cheesecake

For an elegant finish, ring the cake top with rosettes of sweetened whipped cream and then sprinkle them with nutmeg.

FOR THE CRUST:

1 cup (4 oz/125 g) pecan halves

1 cup (3 oz/90 g) graham cracker crumbs

¼ cup (2 oz/60 g) firmly packed brown sugar

5 tablespoons (2½ oz/75 g) unsalted butter, melted and cooled

FOR THE FILLING:

2 lb (1 kg) cream cheese, at room temperature

1 cup (8 oz/250 g) granulated sugar

3 tablespoons Cognac or dark rum

2 teaspoons vanilla extract (essence)

¾ teaspoon ground nutmeg

4 large eggs, at room temperature

2 tablespoons confectioners' (icing) sugar, optional

Position a rack in the middle of an oven and preheat to 350°F (180°C). Spread the pecans on a baking sheet and place in the oven until lightly toasted and fragrant, about 10 minutes. Let cool. Leave the oven set at 350°F (180°C).

In a food processor fitted with the metal blade, combine the toasted pecans, the graham cracker crumbs and brown sugar and process to grind finely. Add the melted butter and process until the crumbs begin to stick together. With your hand draped with plastic wrap to form a glove, press the crumbs firmly onto the bottom and 2 inches (5 cm) up the sides of a springform pan 9 inches (23 cm) in diameter and 2½ inches (6 cm) deep. Wrap aluminum foil around the outside of the pan. Bake the crust for 10 minutes until set. Remove from the oven and let cool. Leave the oven set at 350°F (180°C).

To make the filling, in a large bowl, combine the cream cheese and sugar. Using an electric mixer set on medium speed, beat until well blended. Beat in the Cognac or rum, vanilla and nutmeg. Add the eggs, one at a time, beating after each addition just until combined. Pour the filling into the cooled crust.

Bake until the center 2 inches (5 cm) still quiver slightly when the pan is shaken, about 1 hour. Transfer to a rack and let cool. Cover with aluminum foil and refrigerate overnight or for up to 3 days.

To serve, run a knife around the pan sides to loosen the cake. Remove the foil from the pan and release the pan sides. Place the cheesecake on a plate. Using a fine-mesh sieve, sift the confectioners' sugar over the top just before serving, if desired.

Makes one 9-inch (23-cm) cake; serves 12

Boysenberry–Vanilla Bean Cheesecake Tartlets

FOR THE CRUST:

2¼ cups (7 oz/220 g) graham cracker crumbs

⅓ cup (2½ oz/75 g) firmly packed brown sugar

½ cup (4 oz/125 g) plus 1 tablespoon unsalted butter, melted and cooled

FOR THE FILLING:

1 lb (500 g) cream cheese, at room temperature

½ cup (4 oz/125 g) granulated sugar

1 teaspoon vanilla extract (essence)

1 vanilla bean, cut in half lengthwise

½ cup (4 fl oz/125 ml) heavy (double) cream

1 tablespoon water

½ teaspoon unflavored gelatin

FOR THE TOPPING:

⅓ cup (4 oz/125 g) seedless boysenberry or blackberry jam

3 cups (12 oz/375 g) boysenberries

Preheat an oven to 350°F (180°C). To make the crust, in a food processor fitted with the metal blade, combine the graham cracker crumbs, brown sugar and melted butter. Process until the crumbs begin to stick together. With your hand draped with plastic wrap to form a glove, firmly press about ⅓ cup (1½ oz/45 g) of the crumbs onto the bottom and sides of 8 tartlet pans with removable bottoms 4½ inches (11.5 cm) in diameter. Bake the crusts for 8 minutes until set. Remove from the oven, let cool, then refrigerate until cold.

To make the filling, in a large bowl, combine the cream cheese, granulated sugar and vanilla. Using an electric mixer set on medium speed, beat until well blended. Using a sharp knife, scrape the seeds from the vanilla bean directly into the cream cheese mixture. Add the cream and continue to beat on medium speed until fluffy, about 1 minute.

Place the water in a small saucepan. Sprinkle the gelatin over the top and let soften for 5 minutes. Place over low heat and stir until the gelatin dissolves. Add the gelatin mixture to the cream cheese mixture and beat until fluffy, about 1 minute.

Spoon about ⅓ cup (3 fl oz/80 ml) of the filling into each crust and smooth the tops. Cover with aluminum foil and refrigerate for at least 2 hours or for as long as overnight.

Remove the pan sides from the tartlets. To make the topping, in a small, heavy saucepan over medium heat, stir the jam until melted. Remove from the heat and let cool slightly. Arrange the berries atop the tartlets. Using a pastry brush, brush the jam over the berries. Refrigerate for 10 minutes, then serve.

Makes 8 tartlets

White Chocolate Cheesecake

FOR THE CRUST:

1 package (9 oz/280 g) chocolate wafer cookies, broken

¼ cup (2 oz/60 g) granulated sugar

½ cup (4 oz/125 g) unsalted butter, melted and cooled

FOR THE FILLING:

12 oz (375 g) European white chocolate, chopped

1 cup (8 fl oz/250 ml) heavy (double) cream

1½ lb (750 g) cream cheese, at room temperature

¼ cup (1 oz/30 g) confectioners' (icing) sugar

2 teaspoons vanilla extract (essence)

large block European white chocolate, slightly softened

Serve with sweetened sliced strawberries alongside, if desired. Decorating the top of the cake with white chocolate curls makes this cheesecake even more appealing.

To make the crust, in a food processor fitted with the metal blade, combine the cookies and sugar. Process to grind finely. Add the melted butter and process until the crumbs begin to stick together. With your hand draped with plastic wrap to form a glove, press the crumbs firmly onto the bottom and 2 inches (5 cm) up the sides of a springform pan 9 inches (23 cm) in diameter and 2½ inches (6 cm) deep. Set aside.

To make the filling, in a heavy saucepan over medium heat, combine the white chocolate and cream and heat, stirring constantly, until melted and smooth. Remove from the heat and refrigerate, stirring occasionally, until cool, about 30 minutes.

In a large bowl, combine the cream cheese, confectioners' sugar and vanilla extract. Using an electric mixer set on medium speed, beat until well blended. Add the cooled white chocolate mixture and beat until light and fluffy, about 2 minutes. Pour the filling into the crust and smooth the top with a rubber spatula. Cover with aluminum foil and refrigerate overnight or for up to 3 days.

To serve, run a knife around the pan sides to loosen the cake. Release the pan sides and place the cheesecake on a plate. Cut the white chocolate into long, thin curls (see glossary, page 104). Mound the curls atop the cake and cut into wedges.

Makes one 9-inch (23-cm) cake; serves 12

Peanut Butter Cheesecake

FOR THE CRUST:

1 cup (6 oz/185 g) unsalted roasted peanuts

1 cup (3 oz/90 g) graham cracker crumbs

⅓ cup (2½ oz/75 g) firmly packed brown sugar

¼ cup (2 oz/60 g) unsalted butter, melted and cooled

FOR THE FILLING:

1 lb (500 g) cream cheese, at room temperature

2 cups (1¼ lb/625 g) super-chunky peanut butter

2½ cups (10 oz/315 g) confectioners' (icing) sugar

1 teaspoon vanilla extract (essence)

1 cup (8 fl oz/250 ml) heavy (double) cream, chilled

bittersweet chocolate glaze for topping cheesecake (*recipe on page 15*)

Use only hydrogenated peanut butter; freshly ground peanut butter will not blend easily with the other ingredients.

Position a rack in the middle of an oven and preheat to 350°F (180°C). To make the crust, in a food processor fitted with the metal blade, combine the peanuts, graham cracker crumbs and brown sugar. Process to grind finely. Add the melted butter and process until the crumbs begin to stick together. With your hand draped with plastic wrap to form a glove, press the crumbs firmly onto the bottom and 2¼ inches (5.5 cm) up the sides of a springform pan 9 inches (23 cm) in diameter and 2½ inches (6 cm) deep. Bake the crust for 10 minutes until set. Remove from the oven and let cool completely.

To make the filling, in a large bowl, combine the cream cheese and peanut butter. Using an electric mixer set on medium speed, beat until well blended. Beat in the confectioners' sugar and vanilla until thoroughly incorporated.

In a medium bowl, using an electric mixer fitted with clean, dry beaters and set on medium-high speed, beat the cream to form stiff peaks. Beat the whipped cream into the peanut butter mixture until thoroughly combined. Spoon the filling into the cooled crust and smooth the top with a rubber spatula. Cover with aluminum foil and refrigerate overnight.

The next day, pour the lukewarm glaze over the top. Re-cover with aluminum foil and refrigerate until the glaze sets, at least 2 hours or for up to 3 days.

To serve, run a knife around the pan sides to loosen the cake. Release the pan sides. Place the cheesecake on a plate and cut into wedges.

Makes one 9-inch (23-cm) cake; serves 12

Triple-Berry Cheesecake

FOR THE CRUST:

2 cups (6 oz/185 g) graham cracker
crumbs

¼ cup (2 oz/60 g) sugar

½ cup (4 oz/125 g) unsalted butter,
melted and cooled

FOR THE FILLING:

2 lb (1 kg) cream cheese, at room
temperature

1 cup (8 oz/250 g) sugar

2 tablespoons fresh lemon juice

2 teaspoons vanilla extract (essence)

4 large eggs, at room temperature

FOR THE TOPPING:

1½ cups (12 fl oz/375 ml) sour cream

3 tablespoons sugar

⅓ cup (3½ oz/105 g) seedless
raspberry preserves

1 cup (4 oz/125 g) strawberries, stems
removed and sliced

½ cup (2 oz/60 g) raspberries

½ cup (2 oz/60 g) blueberries

*P*osition a rack in the middle of an oven and preheat to 350°F (180°C). To make the crust, in a food processor fitted with the metal blade, combine the crumbs, sugar and melted butter. Process until the crumbs begin to stick together. With your hand draped with plastic wrap to form a glove, press the crumbs firmly onto the bottom and 2¼ inches (5.5 cm) up the sides of a springform pan 9 inches (23 cm) in diameter and 2½ inches (6 cm) deep. Wrap aluminum foil around the outside of the pan. Bake the crust for 10 minutes until set. Remove from the oven and let cool. Leave the oven set at 350°F (180°C).

To make the filling, in a large bowl, combine the cream cheese, sugar, lemon juice and vanilla extract. Using an electric mixer set on medium speed, beat until well blended. Add the eggs, one at a time, beating after each addition just until combined. Pour the filling into the cooled crust.

Bake until the edges are set but the center still quivers slightly when the pan is shaken, about 1 hour and 10 minutes.

Meanwhile, to make the topping, in a bowl, stir together the sour cream and sugar. When the cheesecake is done, spoon the sour cream mixture over the top. Return the cake to the oven for 5 minutes longer to set. Transfer to a rack to cool. Cover with aluminum foil and refrigerate overnight or for up to 2 days.

The next day, run a knife around the pan sides to loosen the cake. In a large, heavy frying pan over medium heat, stir the preserves until melted. Remove from the heat, add all the berries and toss to coat. Mound the berries atop the cake. Refrigerate for 30 minutes or for up to 2 hours.

To serve, remove the foil from the pan and release the pan sides. Place the cheesecake on a plate and cut into wedges.

Makes one 9-inch (23-cm) cake; serves 12

Espresso-Spice Cheesecake

FOR THE CRUST:

1 package (9 oz/280 g) chocolate wafer
cookies, broken

¼ cup (2 oz/60 g) sugar

½ cup (4 oz/125 g) unsalted butter,
melted and cooled

FOR THE FILLING:

2 tablespoons instant espresso powder

1 tablespoon boiling water

2 lb (1 kg) cream cheese, at room
temperature

1⅓ cups (11 oz/345 g) sugar

¼ cup (2 fl oz/60 ml) heavy
(double) cream

1½ teaspoons ground cinnamon

½ teaspoon ground allspice

4 large eggs, at room temperature

2 teaspoons unsweetened cocoa

*For coffee lovers only! Offer freshly brewed espresso or
cappuccino to go along with this sophisticated dessert.*

To make the crust, in a food processor fitted with the
metal blade, combine the cookies and sugar. Process to
grind finely. Add the melted butter and process until the
crumbs begin to stick together. With your hand draped
with plastic wrap to form a glove, press the crumbs firmly
onto the bottom and 2 inches (5 cm) up the sides of a
springform pan 9 inches (23 cm) in diameter and 2½
inches (6 cm) deep. Wrap aluminum foil around the
outside of the pan.

Position a rack in the middle of an oven and preheat to
350°F (180°C). To make the filling, in a tiny cup, dissolve
the espresso powder in the boiling water. In a large bowl,
combine the cream cheese and sugar. Using an electric
mixer set on medium speed, beat until well blended and
smooth. Beat in the dissolved espresso, the cream,
cinnamon and allspice. Add the eggs, one at a time, beating
after each addition just until combined and stopping
occasionally to scrape down the sides of the bowl. Pour the
filling into the crust.

Bake until the top appears set, about 1 hour. Transfer to
a rack and let cool. Cover with aluminum foil and
refrigerate overnight or for up to 3 days.

To serve, run a knife around the pan sides to loosen the
cake. Remove the foil from the pan and release the pan
sides. Place the cheesecake on a plate and, using a fine-
mesh sieve, sift the cocoa over the top just before serving.

Makes one 9-inch (23-cm) cake; serves 12

Caramel-Pecan Cheesecake

FOR THE CRUST:

2 cups (8 oz/230 g) pecan halves, lightly toasted (*see glossary, page 106*) and cooled

⅓ cup (2½ oz/75 g) firmly packed brown sugar

3 tablespoons unsalted butter, melted and cooled

FOR THE FILLING:

2 lb (1 kg) cream cheese, at room temperature

1 cup (7 oz/220 g) firmly packed brown sugar

2 teaspoons vanilla extract (essence)

1 cup (8 fl oz/250 ml) heavy (double) cream, chilled

1 tablespoon water

1 teaspoon unflavored gelatin

FOR THE TOPPING:

5 tablespoons (2½ oz/75 g) unsalted butter

⅓ cup (2½ oz/75 g) firmly packed brown sugar

⅓ cup (3 fl oz/80 ml) heavy (double) cream

1 cup (4 oz/125 g) pecan halves, lightly toasted (*see glossary, page 106*) and cooled

Preheat an oven to 350°F (180°C). To make the crust, in a food processor fitted with the metal blade, combine the toasted pecans and the brown sugar. Process to grind finely. Add the melted butter and use on-off pulses just until combined. With your hand draped with plastic wrap to form a glove, press the crumbs onto the bottom (but not the sides) of a springform pan 9 inches (23 cm) in diameter and 2½ inches (6 cm) deep. Bake the crust for 10 minutes until set. Remove from the oven and let cool.

To make the filling, in a large bowl, combine the cream cheese, brown sugar and vanilla extract. Using an electric mixer set on medium speed, beat until well blended. Beat in ½ cup (4 fl oz/125 ml) of the cream until thoroughly incorporated.

Place the water in a small saucepan. Sprinkle the gelatin over the top and let soften for 5 minutes. Place over low heat and stir until the gelatin dissolves. Gradually whisk in the remaining ½ cup (4 fl oz/125 ml) cream. Then add the gelatin mixture to the cream cheese mixture and beat until fluffy, about 1 minute. Spoon the filling into the cooled crust. Cover with aluminum foil and refrigerate overnight.

The next day, make the topping: In a small, heavy saucepan over low heat, combine the butter, brown sugar and cream and stir until the sugar dissolves. Raise the heat to high and bring to a boil. Add the toasted pecans and boil, stirring occasionally, until the nuts are thinly coated, about 2 minutes. Let cool slightly and spoon over the cake. Re-cover with aluminum foil and refrigerate until firm, at least 2 hours or for up to 2 days.

To serve, run a knife around the pan sides to loosen the cake. Release the pan sides. Place the cake on a plate; cut into wedges.

Makes one 9-inch (23-cm) cake; serves 12

Chocolate-Mint Cheesecake

FOR THE CRUST:

1 package (9 oz/280 g) chocolate wafer
cookies, broken
¼ cup (2 oz/60 g) sugar
½ cup (4 oz/125 g) unsalted butter,
melted and cooled

FOR THE FILLING:

10 oz (315 g) bittersweet chocolate,
chopped
2 lb (1 kg) cream cheese, at room
temperature
1¼ cups (10 oz/315 g) sugar
⅓ cup (1 oz/30 g) unsweetened cocoa
1 teaspoon peppermint extract (essence)
4 large eggs, at room temperature

fresh mint leaves

*For a pretty decoration, pipe whipped cream around the top edge
of the cake, then garnish with fresh mint leaves.*

To make the crust, in a food processor fitted with the metal
blade, combine the cookies and sugar. Process to form fine
crumbs. Add the melted butter and process until the crumbs
begin to stick together. With your hand draped with plastic
wrap to form a glove, press the crumbs firmly onto the bottom
and all the way up the sides of a springform pan 9 inches
(23 cm) in diameter and 2½ inches (6 cm) deep. Wrap
aluminum foil around the outside of the pan.

Position a rack in the middle of an oven and preheat to 350°F
(180°C).

To make the filling, in a heavy saucepan over very low heat,
melt the chocolate, stirring constantly, until smooth. Remove
from the heat and set aside.

In a large bowl, combine the cream cheese and sugar. Using
an electric mixer set on medium speed, beat until well blended
and smooth. Beat in the cocoa and peppermint extract. Add
the eggs, one at a time, beating after each addition just until
combined. Add the melted chocolate and beat just until
smooth, stopping occasionally to scrape down the sides of the
bowl. Pour the filling into the crust (it will almost fill it).

Bake until the center is just set, about 50 minutes. Transfer
to a rack and let cool. Cover with aluminum foil and refrigerate
overnight or for up to 4 days.

To serve, run a knife around the pan sides to loosen the cake.
Remove the foil from the pan and release the pan sides. Place
the cheesecake on a plate and garnish with mint leaves. Cut
into wedges.

Makes one 9-inch (23-cm) cake; serves 12

Glossary

The following glossary defines terms specifically as they relate to cakes, cupcakes and cheesecakes, including major and unusual ingredients and basic techniques.

ALLSPICE
Sweet spice of Caribbean origin with a flavor suggesting a blend of **cinnamon**, **cloves** and **nutmeg**, hence its name. May be purchased as whole dried berries or ground. When using whole berries, they may be bruised—gently crushed with the bottom of a pan or other heavy instrument—to release more of their flavor.

BAKING POWDER
Commercial baking product combining three ingredients: **baking soda**, the source of the carbon-dioxide gas that causes some cakes to rise; an acid, such as **cream of tartar**, calcium acid phosphate or sodium aluminum sulphate, which causes the baking soda to release its gas when the powder is combined with a liquid; and a starch such as **cornstarch** or flour, to keep the powder from absorbing moisture.

BAKING SODA
Also known as bicarbonate of soda or sodium bicarbonate, the active component of **baking powder** and the source of the carbon dioxide gas that leavens some cakes. Often used on its own to leaven batters that include acidic ingredients such as **buttermilk**, yogurt or citrus juices.

BUTTER, UNSALTED
For cake making, unsalted butter is preferred. To soften butter, let it stand at room temperature for at least 30 minutes before use.

Or place it unwrapped on a microwaveproof plate or in a bowl, or wrap in waxed paper or plastic wrap, and put it in a microwave oven; with the oven set on high, heat the butter for 20 seconds, stopping to check its consistency and repeating as necessary until it is soft enough to mash easily with a fork.

BUTTERMILK
Form of cultured lowfat or nonfat milk that contributes a tangy flavor and thick, creamy texture to some cakes. Its acidity also provides a boost to leavening agents, adding extra lightness to batters.

CHOCOLATE WAFER COOKIES
Any of several commercial varieties of thin, crisp, chocolate-flavored cookies sold in food stores. They may be crushed as an ingredient in crusts for cheesecakes.

CINNAMON
Popular sweet spice for flavoring baked goods. The aromatic bark of a type of evergreen tree, it is sold as whole dried strips— cinnamon sticks—or already ground.

CLOVES
Rich and aromatic East African spice used whole or in its ground form to flavor both sweet and savory recipes.

COCOA, UNSWEETENED
Richly flavored, fine-textured powder ground from the solids left after much of the cocoa butter has been extracted from chocolate liquor. Cocoa powder specially treated to reduce its natural acidity, resulting in a darker color and more mellow flavor, is known as Dutch-process cocoa.

COCONUT
For baking purposes, shredded or flaked coconut is sold ready-to-use in cans or plastic packages in the baking section of most food stores. The label indicates whether the product is sweetened or unsweetened; most cake

---

CHOCOLATE
When making cakes, buy the best-quality chocolate you can find. Many cooks prefer the quality of European chocolate made in Switzerland, Belgium, France or Italy.

Bittersweet Chocolate
Lightly sweetened eating or baking chocolate that generally contains about 40 percent cocoa butter. For superior quality, look for bittersweet chocolate that contains at least 50 percent cocoa butter.

Semisweet Chocolate
Eating or baking chocolate that is usually—but not always—slightly sweeter than bittersweet chocolate. Bittersweet chocolate may be substituted.

White Chocolate
A chocolatelike product for eating or baking, made by combining pure cocoa butter with sugar, powdered milk and sometimes vanilla. Check labels to make sure that the white chocolate you buy is made exclusively with cocoa butter, without the addition of coconut oil or vegetable shortening.

Chocolate Chips
Any of several kinds of chocolate—usually semisweet, bittersweet, milk or white— molded into small drop shapes, for uniform incorporation into batters.

To Make Chocolate Curls
Curls of chocolate make an attractive decoration for cakes and cheesecakes.

To make curls, set a large block of imported chocolate in a warm place until slightly softened. Then, firmly drag the sharp edge of a large knife across the surface of the block to form long, thin curls.

recipes call for sweetened coconut. Canned sweetened cream of coconut, a rich concentrate of the fruit's liquid and fat, is also readily available in the baking or liquor section.

Some recipes call for toasting shredded or flaked coconut to develop its flavor: Spread the coconut evenly on a baking sheet and bake in a 350°F (180°C) oven, stirring occasionally, until pale gold, about 8 minutes.

COFFEE, INSTANT POWDER
Although coffee is best enjoyed as a beverage when freshly brewed from ground coffee beans, any of the many commercial brands of instant coffee and espresso powders may be used as a source of coffee flavor in cake batters and frostings.

CORN SYRUP
Neutral-tasting syrup extracted from corn. Sold either as unfiltered dark corn syrup or filtered light corn syrup

CORNMEAL
Granular flour, ground from the dried kernels of yellow or white corn, with a sweet, robust flavor that is particularly appealing in baked goods. Sometimes known by the Italian term polenta.

CORNSTARCH
Fine, powdery flour ground from the endosperm of corn—the white heart of the kernel. Used as a thickening agent and, because it contains no gluten, to give a delicate texture to baked goods. Also known as cornflour.

CRANBERRIES
Round, deep red, tart berries, grown primarily in wet, sandy coastal lands—or bogs—in the northeastern United States.

CREAM CHEESE
Smooth, white, mild-tasting cheese made from cream and milk, used on its own as a spread or as an ingredient that adds rich flavor and texture to cheesecakes and cake frostings.

Some recipes call for cream cheese that has been softened to room temperature to facilitate its blending with other ingredients. To soften cream cheese quickly, place it unwrapped on a microwaveproof plate and heat in a microwave oven set on high for 20 seconds, stopping to check its consistency and repeating until soft enough to mash easily with a fork.

Alternatively, if the cheese is enclosed in an airtight commercial wrapper, leave the cheese in its wrapper; immerse it in a bowl of hot water until the desired consistency is reached, 2–3 minutes.

CREAM, HEAVY
Whipping cream with a butterfat content of at least 36 percent. For the best flavor and cooking properties, use 100 percent natural fresh cream with a short shelf life printed on the carton, avoiding long-lasting varieties that have been processed by ultraheat methods. In Britain, use double cream.

CREAM, SOUR
Commercial dairy product, made from pasteurized sweet cream, with a tangy flavor and thick consistency.

CREAM OF TARTAR
Acidic powder extracted during wine making that is used as a leavening agent, most commonly combined with **baking soda** to make commercial **baking powder**, to stabilize beaten egg whites and as an ingredient in sugar syrups to prevent crystallization.

EGGS
Eggs are sold in the United States in a range of sizes from jumbo to small. For the recipes in this book, use large eggs.

Separating Eggs
To separate an egg, crack the shell in half by tapping it against the side of a bowl and then breaking it apart with your fingers. Holding the shell halves over the bowl, gently transfer the whole yolk back and forth between them, letting the clear white drop away into the bowl. Take care not to cut into the yolk with the edges of the shell (the whites will not beat properly if they contain any yolk). Transfer the yolk to another bowl.

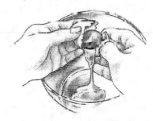

Alternatively, gently pour the egg from the shell onto the slightly cupped fingers of your outstretched (clean) hand, held over a bowl. Let the whites fall between your fingers into the bowl; the whole yolk will remain in your hand.

The same basic function is also performed by an aluminum, ceramic or plastic egg separator placed over a bowl. The separator holds the yolk intact in its cuplike center while allowing the white to drip out through slots in its side into the bowl.

DRIED AND CANDIED FRUIT
Intensely flavored and satisfyingly chewy, many forms of sun-dried or kiln-dried fruits, as well as candied fruits, may be added to enhance the taste or texture of baked goods. Select more recently dried and packaged fruits, which have a softer texture than older dried fruits. Those used in this book are:

Candied Orange Peel and Pineapple
Two of the most popular forms of candied fruit for baking, these are made by saturating pieces of orange peel or pineapple with a sugar syrup, then drying them.

Cherries
Ripe, tart red cherries that have been pitted and dried—usually in a kiln, with a little sugar added to help preserve them—to a consistency and shape similar to raisins.

Dates
Sweet, deep brown fruit of the date palm tree, with a thick, sticky consistency resembling that of candied fruit. Sometimes sold already pitted and chopped.

Figs
Compact form of the succulent black or golden summertime fruit, distinguished by a slightly crunchy texture derived from its tiny seeds.

EXTRACTS
Flavorings derived by dissolving essential oils of richly flavored foods—such as almond, anise, peppermint and **vanilla**—in an alcohol base. Use only products labeled "pure" or "natural" extract (essence) unless using coconut extract, which is only produced in imitation form.

FLOUR, ALL-PURPOSE
Some cake recipes call specifically for all-purpose flour (also known as plain flour), a blend of hard and soft wheats. All-purpose flour is sold in its natural, pale yellow unbleached form or bleached, the result of a chemical process that not only whitens it but also makes it easier to blend with higher percentages of fat and sugar. Bleached all-purpose flour is therefore commonly used for recipes where more tender results are desired, while unbleached all-purpose flour yields more crisp results.

FLOUR, CAKE
A very fine-textured bleached flour, cake flour (also called soft-wheat flour) is the most common flour for making cakes. **All-purpose** (plain) **flour** is not an acceptable substitute.

GELATIN, UNFLAVORED
Unflavored commercial gelatin gives delicate body to some cheesecake fillings. Sold in envelopes holding about 1 tablespoon (¼ oz/7 g).

GINGER
The rhizome of the tropical ginger plant, which yields a sweet, strong-flavored spice. Ginger pieces are available crystallized or candied in specialty-food shops or the baking or Asian sections of well-stocked food stores. Ginger preserved in syrup is sold in specialty shops or in Asian food sections. Ground, dried ginger is easily found in jars or tins in the spice section.

GINGERSNAPS
Any of several commercial varieties of thin, crisp, ginger-flavored cookies sold in food stores. They may be crushed as an ingredient in cheesecake crusts.

GRAHAM CRACKERS
Crisp, sweet crackers made from whole-wheat flour and usually honey. Cookies in their own right, they are often crumbled or crushed for use in cheesecake crusts.

HONEY
The natural, sweet, syruplike substance produced by bees from flower nectar. Honey subtly reflects the color, taste and aroma of the blossoms from which it was made. Milder varieties, such as clover and orange blossom, are lighter in color and better suited to general cooking purposes. Honey provides a distinctive mellow sweetness in cake and cheesecake recipes.

NUTS
Flavorful, crunchy nuts complement a variety of cake and cheesecake recipes.

To toast nuts, spread them on a baking sheet and place in a 350°F (180°C) oven until lightly toasted (8 minutes for sliced almonds or macadamias; 10 minutes for hazelnuts, pecans or walnuts).

Almonds
Mellow, sweet-flavored nuts that are an important crop in California and are popular throughout the world.

Hazelnuts
Small, usually spherical nuts with a slightly sweet flavor. Grown in Italy, Spain and the United States. Also known as filberts.

Macadamias
Spherical nuts, about twice the diameter of hazelnuts, with a very rich, buttery flavor and crisp texture. Native to Australia, they are now grown primarily in Hawaii.

Peanuts
Not true nuts, these are actually legumes produced on a low-branching plant. When roasted, they have a rich, full flavor and satisfying crispness that make them the world's most popular nut. The Virginia variety is longer and more oval than the smaller, rounder, red-skinned Spanish peanut. Native to South America, peanuts are an important crop in Africa and the United States.

Pecans
Brown-skinned, crinkly textured nuts with a distinctive sweet, rich flavor and crisp, slightly crumbly texture. Native to the southern United States.

Pistachios
Slightly sweet, full-flavored nuts with distinctively green, crunchy meat. Native to Asia Minor, they are grown primarily in the Middle East and California.

Walnuts
Rich, crisp-textured nuts with distinctively crinkled surfaces. English walnuts, the most familiar variety, are grown worldwide, although the largest crops are in California. American black walnuts, sold primarily as shelled pieces, have a stronger flavor that lends extra distinction to desserts and candies.

MARSALA
Dry or sweet amber Italian wine from the area of Marsala, in Sicily; widely used to flavor both sweet and savory dishes.

MASCARPONE
A thick Italian cream cheese, usually sold in tubs and similar to French crème fraîche. Look for mascarpone in the cheese case of an Italian delicatessen or a specialty-food shop.

MOLASSES
Thick, robust-tasting, syrupy sugarcane by-product of sugar refining. Light molasses results from the first boiling of the syrup; dark molasses from the second boiling.

NECTAR, FRUIT
Canned or bottled juicelike beverage combining fruit juice or pulp with sugar and water to make a thick, sweet drink. Peach and pear nectars are among the most common varieties.

NUTMEG
Popular baking spice that is the hard pit of the fruit of the nutmeg tree. May be bought already ground or, for fresher flavor, whole. Whole nutmeg can be grated as needed using a nutmeg grater.

OILS
Relatively flavorless oils such as safflower, canola and other high-quality mild vegetable oils are used when no taste is desired from the oil—usually the case in cake recipes that derive some richness and texture from oil. Store all oils in airtight containers away from heat and light.

PEANUT BUTTER
A savory paste made from ground peanuts that is often used either as a spread or an ingredient in sauces and baked goods. Hydrogenated peanut butters are generally preferred to freshly ground varieties for use in cheesecakes because they blend easily with other ingredients and their oils do not separate.

PEPPERMINT EXTRACT
Flavoring derived by dissolving the essential oil of fresh peppermint leaves in an alcohol base. Use only products labeled "pure" or "natural" peppermint extract (essence).

PUMPKIN PURÉE
Seedless orange-colored purée of pumpkin meat often used in pies, cheesecakes and other bakery items. Available canned in most food stores.

POPPYSEEDS
Small, spherical, blue-black seeds of a form of poppy; traditionally used in central and Eastern European cooking to add rich, nutlike flavor to baked goods.

PRESERVES, FRUIT
In comparison to clear fruit jellies and smoother-textured jams, preserves gain distinction from the larger chunks or whole pieces of fruit—such as raspberries, strawberries and apricots—they contain. Preserves make a popular filling for cakes or topping for cheesecakes. Buy the best-quality preserves you can find.

SUGARS
Many different forms of sugar may be used to sweeten cakes and frostings:

Brown Sugar. A rich-tasting granulated sugar combined with molasses in varying quantities to yield golden, light or dark brown sugar, with crystals varying from coarse to finely granulated. To measure brown sugar accurately, pack it firmly and evenly into measuring cups or spoons.

Confectioners' Sugar. Finely pulverized sugar, also known as powdered or icing sugar, which dissolves quickly and provides a thin, white decorative coating. To prevent confectioners' sugar from absorbing moisture in the air and caking, manufacturers often mix **cornstarch** into it.

Granulated Sugar. The standard, widely used form of pure white sugar. Do not use superfine granulated sugar (or castor sugar) unless specified.

VANILLA BEAN
Vanilla beans are dried aromatic pods of a variety of orchid; one of the most popular flavorings in dessert making. Vanilla is most commonly used in the form of an alcohol-based **extract** (essence); be sure to purchase products labeled "pure vanilla extract." Vanilla extract or beans from Madagascar are the best.

To remove the seeds from a vanilla bean, use a small, sharp knife to cut the bean in half lengthwise. Then, with the tip of the knife, scrape out the tiny seeds within each of the bean's halves.

ZEST
Thin, brightly colored, outermost layer of a citrus fruit's peel, containing most of its aromatic essential oils—a lively source of flavor in baking. Zest may be removed using one of two easy methods:

1. Use a simple tool known as a zester, drawing its sharp-edged holes across the fruit's skin to remove the zest in thin strips. Alternatively, use a fine hand-held grater.

2. Holding the edge of a paring knife or vegetable peeler away from you and almost parallel to the fruit's skin, carefully cut off the zest in thin strips, taking care not to remove any of the bitter white pith with it. Then thinly slice or chop the strips on a cutting board.

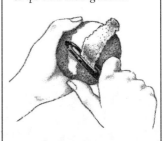

Index

ACKNOWLEDGMENTS

The publishers would like to thank the following people and organizations for
their generous assistance and support in producing this book:
William Garry, Kristine Kidd, Todd Taverner, Henry and Nancy Tenaglia, Annie and Mike Denn, Sharon C. Lott,
Stephen W. Griswold, Ken DellaPenta, Claire Sanchez, Tarji Mickelson, Jennifer Hauser,
Jennifer Mullins, and the buyers and store managers for Pottery Barn and Williams-Sonoma stores.

The following kindly lent props for the photography: Biordi Art Imports, Candelier, Fredericksen Hardware, Sandra Griswold,
Fillamento, Forrest Jones, Sue Fisher King, Susan Massey, RH Shop, Waterford/Wedgwood and Chuck Williams.